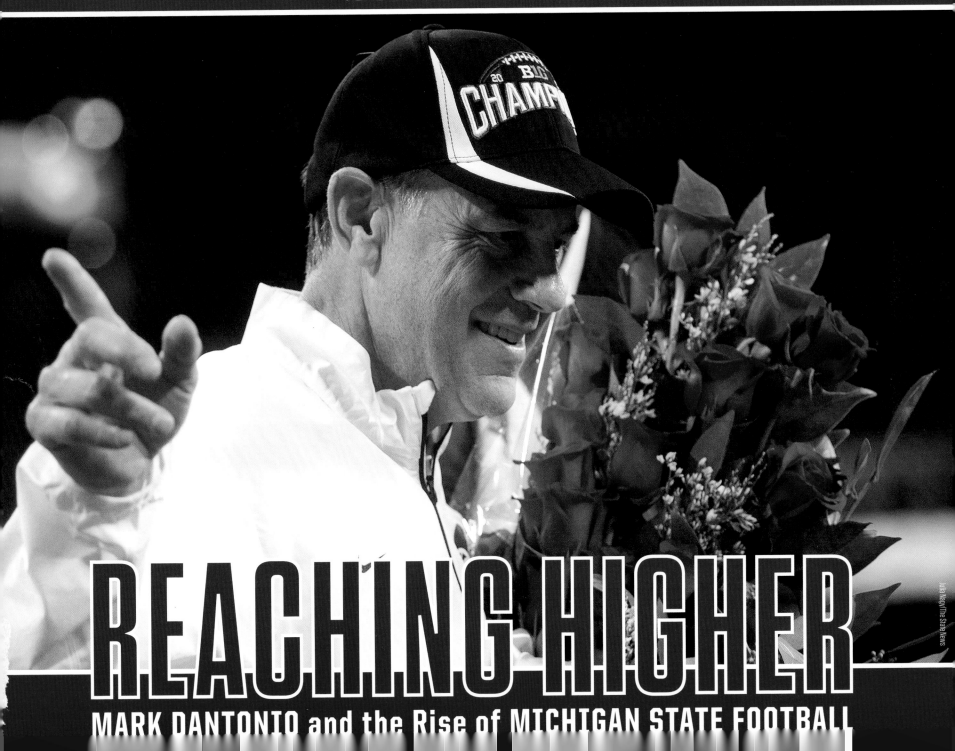

REACHING HIGHER

MARK DANTONIO and the Rise of MICHIGAN STATE FOOTBALL

This book is available in quantity at special discounts for your group or organization.

For further information, contact:

Triumph Books LLC
814 North Franklin Street
Chicago, Illinois 60610
Phone: (312) 337-0747
www.triumphbooks.com

Printed in U.S.A.

ISBN: 978-1-62937-320-1

The State News
General Manager: Marty Sturgeon
Editorial Advisors: Robert Hendricks, Omar Sofradzija

The State News would like to gratefully acknowledge the effort of the student staff of reporters and
photographers who contributed to the coverage of Michigan State football between 2007-2015.

Content packaged by Mojo Media, Inc.
Jason Hinman: Creative Director
Joe Funk: Editor

Front cover photo by Angeli Wright/The State News
Back cover top left and bottom left photos by Julia Nagy/The State News
Back cover top center and top right photos by Josh Radtke/The State News
Back cover bottom center photo by Matt Radick/The State News
Back cover bottom right photo by James Ristau/The State News

Contents

Introduction

By Ryan Kryska

In the early phases of the 20th century, Michigan Agricultural College was looking for a new place to play football. The first thing that needed to be done was the mapping of a field. Builders marked a patch of grass and gave it football's 100 yards of length and 53 yards of width. Next, the sidelines, yard markers, numbers and goal posts came to life under the labor of early Spartans. In between these lines, you'd find the essence of football — the sweet smell of freshly cut grass and the sound of colliding pads during a summer two-a-day practice. Outside of these lines, the spectacle was on its way. Fourteen thousand people could watch between the lines of the then-College Field in 1923. Now fast forward to 1956, when Spartan Stadium became home to a crowd of 76,000. And then again, to 2007, when the entire stadium was stripped bare to what lay between those lines.

The builders of that original field — the original marks — in between the lines and walled off from the spectacle, came back. And this is where Mark Dantonio's story begins.

His philosophy restored the essence of football at Michigan State University. The smell of that grass and the colliding of those pads once again became the cornerstone. A program in flux was no more, it was stable, and a team-first mindset was restored.

On the next 144 pages, you will find the story of how Dantonio arrived, built and sustained a broken MSU football program. Through the eyes of *The State News'* writers and photographers his story is told each step of the way with a first-hand point of view. The trick plays, the miraculous finishes and the consistent success through a college football era of parity comes to life with each turn of the page. I am just one of these writers that got to know Coach, and more will follow as his tenure continues.

In early 2015, I was handed a "Reach Higher" media notepad. Inside is an infographic titled "The Dantonio Era." It reads: "53 wins since 2010 — most in Big Ten and seventh most in FBS. Eight school-record consecutive bowl appearances, including four straight wins. Four double-digit win seasons in last five years. Two back-to-back top-five finishes (No. 3 in 2013, No. 5 in 2014). Only school to win BCS game and New Year's Six bowl the last two seasons. A winning percentage of .708."

Over the following months, I would fill this notepad with quotes, questions, highlights and statistics of a season that included the miracle in The Big House and a trip to the College Football Playoff Cotton Bowl. When 2016 rolled around, and it was time to hang up my hat, I was faced with a question. Do I retire this notepad, and keep it as my personal memoir, or do I continue to write on the 20-plus pages still left blank?

And then the answer became clear. I would continue. Because even though his first 90 pages were the greatest years of this writer's life, Dantonio's 100th page and beyond has yet to be written. ∎

Ryan Kryska covered the 2015 MSU football team as a writer for The State News.

Head coach Mark Dantonio congratulates junior wide receiver R.J. Shelton on his touchdown in the second quarter of MSU's 2015 Homecoming win over Purdue.
Julia Nagy/The State News

Coaching Decision Good Call For MSU

By Steve Highfield • November 28, 2006

Don't look now, but MSU got it right. During the almost monthlong coaching search since John L. Smith was fired, there's been pessimism, uncertainty and speculation surrounding the hiring process.

It's taking too long.

Politics within the administration will be the downfall of this hire.

MSU will make the same old mistakes.

And who could blame people expressing those sentiments? Hindsight proved that both John L. Smith and his predecessor, Bobby Williams, were the wrong hires.

But on Monday, MSU President Lou Anna K. Simon swung a swift ax through the roots of those doubts when she introduced Mark Dantonio as MSU's next football coach.

Critics still have their theories that Dantonio was the compromise pick after Simon wanted Central Michigan coach Brian Kelly and others involved in the search preferred Cleveland Browns defensive coordinator Todd Grantham.

But in a process filled with conspiracy theories and alleged sources embedded deep within the university, I instead employ common sense. If Dantonio wasn't in fact an initial leading candidate, how is a contract in place for him approximately 19 hours after the first interview with him was conducted?

The fact is, MSU interviewed him late in the process because that's what was mandated by Dantonio's situation. His Cincinnati team played its last regular season game Saturday, and, out of respect, he didn't want to interview or comment prior to regular season's end.

None of that implies Dantonio came out of nowhere.

"I had a pretty good sense that I was a finalist early on," Dantonio said. "It was just a matter of whether they were going to wait and interview me or not. Michigan State did it the right way."

The right way meant MSU's four-man interview team — Ron Mason, Mark Hollis, Tom Izzo and former MSU football player and current MSU police Lt. Alan Haller — departed for Cincinnati late Saturday night — after MSU's basketball game against Oakland at Breslin Center — to interview Dantonio.

Simon spoke with Dantonio again Sunday morning, and a five-year contract was in place by Sunday evening.

You may call that move desperation. I call it decisiveness.

He's not the sexiest pick, but he's the right one. A sexy pick might put a spread offense on the field and climb mountains in the offseason, but the right pick instills toughness and a winning attitude in all of his players.

There are few résumés that could have meshed with MSU's coaching wish list better than Dantonio's. He has head coaching experience, putting together an 18-17 record and two bowl berths in three years as Cincinnati's head coach. Before he took the Cincinnati job,

Head coach Mark Dantonio gives direction to senior safety Travis Key in 2007. Dantonio went 7-6 in his first season coaching the Spartans. Sam Ruiz/The State News

he helped put together Ohio State's defense as its defensive coordinator from 2001 to 2003. In 2002, his defense played an integral role in Ohio State winning the national championship.

Still not good enough? Dantonio served as defensive secondary coach for MSU from 1995 to 2000 — a time when MSU actually had a secondary. During those six seasons, seven different MSU defensive backs earned some type of All-Big Ten honors.

He brings all sorts of intangibles to the table. He has a toughness to him, and he demands that toughness and effort be prevalent in all his players. At the same time, he strives to be a coach his players can turn to for off-field help.

He knows about MSU's tradition and says his aim is to "bring all the Spartans together." He's familiar with recruiting in the Midwest and Michigan and has experience recruiting in the South. He is aggressively attacking a job the last two coaches failed at. Perhaps most encouraging of all, he doesn't line up 186-pound wide receivers at quarterback or have a gameplan that involves a bandit.

"I don't think you find a perfect guy," Izzo said. "It's the perfect guy for your fit and the perfect guy that's multidimensional enough to deal with all the things you have to deal with in that situation.

"In that respect, he's the perfect guy."

And who am I to argue with Izzo? ∎

Right: Mark Dantonio yells at his players after junior running back Javon Ringer's 76-yard rush in the third quarter of the Spartans' 28-24 loss against rival Michigan in 2007. Marc Nardacci/The State News Opposite: Mark Dantonio smiles after being drenched in Gatorade by the players. Michigan State earned its seventh and final victory of the 2007 season with a win over Penn State, 35-31. Nick Dentamaro/The State News

100

It's been more than seven years since football head coach Mark Dantonio took the job at MSU. With his 100th game approaching against Indiana on Saturday, he reflects on the progress the program has seen since 2007

By Geoff Preston • October 16, 2014

Nov. 27, 2006, was a day that changed the course of Spartan history forever. It was the day that Mark Dantonio and his staff took over for John L. Smith at MSU.

Nearly eight years, two Big Ten championships and one Rose Bowl title later, in the blink of an eye it has been 99 games under the current regime. Saturday, when No. 8 MSU (5-1 overall, 2-0 Big Ten) goes on the road to face Indiana, (3-3 overall, 0-2 Big Ten) it will be the 100th game for Dantonio at MSU.

It's been a tenure marked by more than a 69-30 record, according to his players and coaching staff. It has been a tenure marked by honesty, excellence and change in the lives of the people on and off the field.

Old faces

In the coaching carousel world of college football, it's rare to find a staff that is able to stay together as long as the staff under Dantonio has.

"Probably the most important thing I did here was select our staff," he said. "The continuity we've had as a staff has been largely responsible for our success both on the playing field and off."

The lack of turnover has helped the staff become better coaches as well. Offensive line coach Mark Staten has been in East Lansing for all 99 previous games and said the staff has become a second family to him.

"You've got nine brothers who are going to help you out," he said. "That's what people don't realize about Mark Dantonio. The stakes are higher than ever since we got here, yet he still keeps his family first."

Staten has been with Dantonio since his days as a defensive coordinator at Ohio State, dating back to 2003. He said when you're with a staff for as long as they have been, sometimes complacency can come into effect, which is not always a good thing.

Coach Dantonio gets fired up after a postgame prayer with his team during the 2013 season. The Spartans were victorious over the Hawkeyes at Kinnick Stadium, 26-14.
Khoa Nguyen/The State News

"Sometimes you can become comfortable, which is good and bad," he said. "You don't want to be too comfortable because you owe it to the people who you've grown together with to keep pushing the envelope."

Staten said it has been fun over the years to watch how the families of the coaches interact.

"We were watching the TV yesterday and my 4-year-old saw Dantonio running around on the TV and he goes 'there's my buddy,'" he said. "It's comfortable. When pieces fit together everything functions better."

Through it all, Dantonio said he never expected to spend 100 games at one place and with his staff mostly intact.

"I really didn't look at 100 games," he said. "That's almost unthinkable when you're starting at No. 1. I think we tried to do it the right way and I think there's been consistency in what we've done."

Player's coach

A coach is only as good as his players, and his players will only play well if they respect their coach. MSU players respect their coach, the man who has been able to take lower-recruited players and make them NFL talents.

A consistent theme when players talk about Dantonio is that he has an honest approach to how he recruits and teaches football.

"The coaching staff preaches and teaches to us hard work, toughness and just beating the man across from you," senior running back Nick Hill said. "One of the things I really admire about coach Dantonio is his honesty. Even when he was recruiting me, he was always honest with me."

The personality of Dantonio can change, according to Hill, from one of quiet composure to the stereotypical screaming football coach.

"At times he'll sit back and let the coaches do their job," he said. "If he needs to step in, he'll step in and be assertive. He has both sides in him."

Sophomore linebacker Riley Bullough is part of the first family of Spartan football. He went to many games at Spartan Stadium as a kid before the success of the program. He said there is a noticeable difference between the culture of the program before and after the hiring of Mark Dantonio.

"I grew up a fan my whole life, and I can say the culture here is completely different from what it used to be," he said. "The staff has been together so long and that's kind of what makes it work. They're really kind of like a family."

Senior offensive lineman Travis Jackson is one of the longest tenured Spartans on the roster. He echoed what his teammates said about Dantonio and his staff being an honest group that preaches hard work.

"It's been a special time to be a Spartan," he said. "When he recruited me, he talked about not only recruiting great players, but recruiting great people, and that was really important because you want to surround yourself with great people in college."

Junior quarterback Connor Cook said that the accomplishments of the staff are important and should be celebrated, but all of the pomp and circumstance doesn't mean a lot if the team doesn't beat Indiana on Saturday.

"We're trying to look at it as another game," he said. "It's another Big Ten game, and that's how we look at it." ■

Mark Dantonio leads his team along Red Cedar Road toward Spartan Stadium before a game against Michigan in 2013. The Spartans defeated the Wolverines, 29-6. Georgina De Moya/The State News

Izzo And Mark Dantonio Have Developed A Close Friendship

By Geoff Preston • November 21, 2014

It's not common for programs to have the success in both basketball and football that MSU has had, which makes it even less common for the two coaches of those teams to be as close as Tom Izzo and Mark Dantonio have become over the years.

Since Dantonio came to East Lansing in 2007, Izzo has taken Dantonio under his wing as the football team has climbed to new heights.

"That was a benefit," Dantonio said.

Dantonio also said he and Izzo have spoken plenty of times about MSU's rivalry with Michigan.

"Me and coach Izzo have talked frequently about this," he said. "We're kind of on the same wave length."

Izzo also said during a taping of the popular ESPN show "First Take" that he was instrumental in getting Dantonio to come from Cincinnati to East Lansing.

"Nick Saban and I came at the same time," Izzo said. "Mark Dantonio came in as an assistant coach and really did an incredible job."

That, according to Izzo, is when their friendship started.

"We became friends, our wives became friends (and) our daughters are the same age," he said.

Izzo said he was one of the people who was able to bring Dantonio into town.

"When he left for Ohio State, I watched him win the national championship there as a defensive coordinator," he said. "Then I watched him go to Cincinnati, and, after the job he did, I got to be one of three or four people that got to interview Mark. Everybody did their job and I played a small part."

Izzo has always had a love for football. He grew up with former NFL head coach Steve Mariucci and said he almost left his basketball assistant coaching position at Northern Michigan for a football coaching position at Cal State Fullerton with Mariucci.

"I almost did go there," he said. "There was a position open there in the defensive backs, which is the position I played, and I love football."

Izzo said in the same interview that he loves MSU's success in football because he can experience the success of a sport he loves. Dantonio has reciprocated the support by coming to many of the Big Ten basketball games inside Breslin Center during his tenure.

Izzo has been to plenty of football games himself, even sitting in the student section following a lightning delay in 2013 against South Florida. ∎

Football coach Mark Dantonio and Spartans basketball coach Tom Izzo catch up at the Breslin Center before MSU tips off against Michigan in 2014. The two elite coaches have established a close relationship during their hugely successful tenures at Michigan State. Julia Nagy/The State News

Dantonio: 'It's not over'

By Jon Schultz • November 5, 2007

Classless. Disrespectful. Mockery. Arrogant.

Those are the words used by the MSU football team to describe how Michigan acted following its 28-24 victory at Spartan Stadium on Saturday.

After the game, U-M players gathered midfield for a moment of silence, intended to mock MSU head coach Mark Dantonio's comment about U-M's loss to Appalachian State. When asked about that loss in a radio interview earlier in the season, Dantonio joked about having a "moment of silence" for the Wolverines.

"I find a lot of the things they do amusing," Dantonio said at his Monday press conference. "They need to check themselves sometimes."

This was not the mild-mannered Dantonio that has shown up to every other weekly press conference of the season.

"Can you tell my tone?" Dantonio asked reporters.

He responded to the postgame comments made by U-M running back Mike Hart, who laughed while calling the Spartans U-M's "little brother."

"Sometimes you get your little brother excited when you're playing basketball, and you let him get the lead," Hart said Saturday after the game, according to the *Detroit Free Press*. "Then you come back and take it back."

Dantonio questioned the ability of the 5-foot-9 running back to even have a "little brother."

"Does Hart have a little brother? Or is he the little brother?" Dantonio said, measuring midway up his chest with his hand. "I don't know."

Dantonio also responded to Hart's claim that he "thought it was funny" when MSU took the lead in the second half.

"Go back and watch their sideline," he said, referring to when MSU had the lead. "I didn't see anybody laughing over there."

Up until this point, if anyone on the

Spartan football team hasn't taken this rivalry personally, they do now, junior quarterback Brian Hoyer said.

He said Hart's comments "just show the classlessness" that he has.

"Sooner or later the little brother, (if) you want to put us that way, you get pushed around enough, the little brother fights back and kicks the other brother's ass," Hoyer said Monday.

"After you make a comment like that, we don't really feel you deserve to win that game. And I'm sure they walked away feeling a little bit lucky coming out of it, too."

During the interview, Dantonio said he'd rather not comment on Hart's remarks. But after a brief pause, he let it out.

"I guess I can't help myself," Dantonio said. "As I said earlier, it's not over. I'm going to be a coach here for a long time. It's not over, it's just starting."

Dantonio said his passion for this rivalry has

Michigan junior tight end Carson Butler (85) fends off senior defensive end Jonal Saint-Dic (94) as senior running back Mike Hart (20) streaks down the sideline. Michigan came away with the coveted Paul Bunyan Trophy in the heated 2007 match-up. Hannah Engelson/The State News

been ingrained in him since he was a defensive backs coach at MSU in 1995.

"It exists in me, and it exists in everybody who is a true Spartan," he said. "Not the ones who give their donor seats to the Michigan Wolverines. It exists in everything. It's there."

While the rivalry sinks deep beneath the skin for Dantonio, many Wolverines downplay the matchup. But senior running back Jehuu Caulcrick said "you would be a fool" to not consider U-M vs. MSU a rivalry game.

"Before the game, people were saying Michigan doesn't consider us a rivalry," Caulcrick said. "They were out there celebrating like they won the championship themselves. Don't let them fool you." ∎

Right: Mark Dantonio shakes hands with Michigan head coach Lloyd Carr after the Spartans' tough 28-24 loss. Jason Chiou/The State News Opposite: Running back Javon Ringer gets pumped up during a timeout in the third quarter. Ringer gained 128 yards against Michigan. Nick Dentamaro/The State News

Senior quarterback Brian Hoyer (7) directs a play during a 21-7 victory against Purdue in 2008. Jeana-Dee Allen/ The State News

Seasoned Hoyer Set To Finish Where He Started

By Jacob Carpenter • November 20, 2008

The MSU football team had little to play for against Penn State on Nov. 18, 2006.

The Spartans were the bottom of program valley, 4-7 with one game remaining, with head coach John L. Smith orchestrating his final game at MSU.

Even with 108,000 fans looking down on the Spartans, nobody had a reason to be nervous.

Except Brian Hoyer.

The sophomore quarterback was making his first career start in what he considered the Big Ten's most imposing monster — Beaver Stadium.

"To play in a place like that on their Senior Day, it made you feel small," Hoyer said.

The North Olmsted, Ohio, native will return to the scene of his debut as a college starter Saturday against Penn State. The stakes, however, are different this season. The Spartans will get at least a share of the Big Ten Championship with a win, and a rowdy Penn State crowd will have an extra edge with a Rose Bowl appearance on the line.

"It's ironic that my first Big Ten game (as a starter) was there and my last Big Ten game will be there," said Hoyer, who completed 30-of-61 passes for 291 yards, one touchdown and zero interceptions at Beaver Stadium.

"It's kind of weird, but at least I have a feel of what type of atmosphere will be there and I'm anxious to get back there and play because there's a lot riding on it."

When Hoyer runs into the huddle for MSU's first drive Saturday, he will have evolved from the anxious sophomore that rallied the Spartans to a near-win in 2006 (the Spartans fell 17-13).

Senior right guard Roland Martin, who started at Penn State with Hoyer, said he could tell Hoyer wasn't nervous in front of the raucous Beaver Stadium crowd two years ago.

"You could look in his eyes and see he was quite motivated and knew what he had to do," said Martin, who has started every game this season. "Hoyer's always the same guy and he's always upbeat and just looking for positive ways to motivate you."

After 16 wins as a starter in two seasons, including a four-touchdown outing in a 35-31 win against the Nittany Lions last season, coaches and players have confidence in the senior.

"I have a huge comfort level just from the fact that Brian Hoyer is our quarterback," MSU head coach Mark Dantonio said. "He's experienced a high level of anxiety in (Beaver Stadium) and that's something that will benefit us greatly and it's a huge advantage for us when one of your leaders has played in that environment and been successful."

After going through the fire of one game at Beaver Stadium, Hoyer knows what goals to aim for in maintaining his composure — avoiding third-and-long situations, staying out of the shadows of the Penn State student section and ignoring the constant catcalls blasted over speakers after every Nittany Lions big play.

"Their student section is really loud, especially when you get in their own end zone," Hoyer said.

"The way their stadium is, it's just kind of a box. It's closed in so the sound really bounces back at you. It's the loudest stadium I've ever played in." ∎

All Grown Up

Spartans take down rivals in the Big House, defeating Wolverines 35-21 in Ann Arbor

By Cash Kruth • October 26, 2008

ANN ARBOR — After MSU's 35-21 victory over Michigan on Saturday, Brian Hoyer and Javon Ringer entered the postgame media room, a square cement area under Michigan Stadium. The room was filled with cameras, media members and a table with three chairs set up under the only decoration in the room: a black, vinyl covering with the U-M block "M" and Big Ten Network logos scattered all over it. "Take it down!" said someone in the media.

Hoyer and Ringer quickly looked at two MSU Athletic Communications directors, who lowered their heads and slowly shook them sideways, in a "Don't even think about it" manner.

The banner stayed up, mainly because everything else that symbolized U-M in the in-state rivalry had come crashing down.

"Eighteen years of coming down here — this is my first time and it's my last time," said Hoyer, a senior quarterback who threw for 282 yards and three touchdowns on 17-for-29 passing.

"That's pretty special. It's a great accomplishment to do this in my last chance."

QUICK HITS
Hero of the game: Blair White

The former walk-on wide receiver from Saginaw had the biggest game of his career on the biggest stage, hauling in four catches for 143 yards and one touchdown. White (or "Whitey" to his teammates) broke a 61-yard slant pass for the game's first touchdown and had two key receptions on MSU's go-ahead touchdown drive.

Goat of the game: Michigan secondary

The U-M secondary, which was touted as part of the Wolverines' strong defense entering the season, surrendered three passes of 40 yards or more and allowed MSU quarterback Brian Hoyer to go 8-of-12 passing on third down. All eight completions were completed either for first downs or touchdowns.

Turning point

With the score tied at 21 midway through the fourth quarter, the Spartans faced a third-and-five with the ball on their own 35-yard line. Hoyer dropped back and hit White over the middle for a clutch 17-yard first down that led to MSU's fourth touchdown five plays later.

Ranked again

The Spartans have returned to the polls after this weekend's win, coming in at No. 22 in the Associated Press Top 25. MSU (7-2 overall, 4-1 Big Ten) dropped out of the AP poll last week

Junior wide receiver Blair White (25) sprints for a 61-yard touchdown from senior quarterback Brian Hoyer. The Spartans prevailed over the Wolverines 35-21 in the 2008 clash in Ann Arbor. Jason Chiou/The State News

"(Michigan defenders) called me Uncle Roland a couple times ... Uncle Roland just gave you a spanking."

— Senior offensive guard Roland Martin on the trash talk between teams during Saturday's game

after its 45-7 blowout loss against Ohio State, but jumped Pittsburgh, Kansas, Georgia Tech and Boston College into the top 25 again.

Hoyer and Ringer, a senior running back, helped break numerous U-M streaks with their performance Saturday.

They become the first MSU team to beat U-M in six years, the first to win in Ann Arbor since 1990 and the first group of seniors in three consecutive classes to beat the Wolverines.

"Being able to go out our senior year with a victory over Michigan to, Lord willing, help (start) a tradition of us beating those guys is great," Ringer said.

Whether or not a string of MSU victories follow Saturday's win remains to be seen, but something all players hope for is that Saturday's outcome will affect how MSU is viewed outside of the program.

Senior defensive tackle Justin Kershaw acknowledged this win was for more than just the seniors and the rest of the Spartans; it spread all over the country to former players and MSU alumni.

Hoyer also said he believed his team's win will affect the way the Spartans are viewed throughout the state of Michigan.

"(MSU offensive coordinator Don Treadwell) talked before the game about making a change," Hoyer said. "We need to make a change in this rivalry and make a change in this state. I think the state is probably more green today than it was yesterday."

Wiley left out

Although Hoyer, Ringer and Kershaw got to fully experience their first victory over the Wolverines, fellow senior captain Otis Wiley was stuck on the sidelines during Saturday's win.

Wiley, MSU's starting strong safety and arguably its best defensive player, didn't practice all week because of a knee injury.

Sophomore Marcus Hyde stepped in for Wiley, garnering four tackles, forcing and recovering a fumble and getting an interception.

"I just wanted to go out there," Hyde said of his first start.

"That's basically what (head coach Mark Dantonio) said: Just go out there and play. If you know what you're doing, the game comes easy at times."

Playing through pain

Ringer and sophomore cornerback Chris L. Rucker also were banged up heading into the game, but still managed to contribute and make plays.

Ringer, who went down during Thursday's practice with a hamstring injury, carried the ball 37 times for 197 yards and two touchdowns in his final game against the Wolverines.

Rucker, still reeling from an injury suffered against Iowa on Oct. 4, had three tackles, a fumble recovery and an interception despite wearing a protective sleeve over his left arm.

"It's good, it's getting better," Rucker said. "I'm not 100 percent yet, but I'll get there real soon. Next week, hopefully I'll be feeling better than I did this week. We're just going to take it week by week." ■

Junior linebacker Brandon Denson (34) and junior safety Jesse Johnson (26) hold up the Paul Bunyan Trophy after defeating the Wolverines 35-21 at Michigan Stadium. The Spartans reclaimed the trophy after a seven-year drought vs Michigan. Jason Chiou/The State News

Senior running back Javon Ringer breaks free from Michigan freshman defensive tackle Mike Martin (68) and sophomore linebacker Jonas Mouton (8) for a 64-yard run.
Jeana-Dee Allen/
The State News

Three Of A Kind

A tough man on the field and a cartoon-loving kid at heart, Javon Ringer isn't your average football star

By Jacob Carpenter • October 16, 2008

It's a mystery how Javon Ringer can be three different people on any given MSU football Saturday. First he's a kid, waking up in a hotel room to watch Saturday morning cartoons before going out to play football with his friends. Give him a few hours and he's an athlete — 5 feet 9 inches of muscle, heart and motor standing tall in the Spartans' backfield. When the game ends and most fans have piled into their cars, he's a humble adult: shaking every hand, signing every autograph, taking every picture before leaving for the night.

In a world of coddled athletes with egos the size of stadiums, the three faces of Ringer on a football Saturday are as fresh as the morning air in the heart of football season. And whether it's the athlete, the adult or the adolescent in Ringer, each face continues to show itself Sunday through Friday.

The athlete

When coaches at Chaminade-Julienne High in Dayton, Ohio, Ringer's alma mater, would forget to blow the whistle to stop a running play during practice, Ringer's teammates would come to a standstill.

He wouldn't. He would keep running. Off the field. Through the parking lot. Through the high school campus.

"Coach, you forgot to blow the whistle," players would say before retrieving the star athlete.

Ringer is a dream tailback. He sprints the 40-yard dash in 4.3 seconds, bench presses 400 pounds — levels typically reserved for linemen — keeps playing until he hears the high-pitched squeal of a coach's whistle, and, according to MSU running backs coach Dan Enos, never has an off day.

Never.

During the summer, when other teammates are running the steps of Spartan Stadium, Ringer is in tow with a 20-pound vest smothering his shoulders and another 20 pounds clinging to his waist.

This year, Ringer is also carrying the extra weight of more carries and expectations on his broad shoulders. But through seven games, his rushing numbers are so far off the charts, they can't be contained by axes.

Getting To Know MSU Running Back Javon Ringer:

- Earned a black belt in karate.
- Can do a roundhouse kick over teammates' heads while in full pads.
- Enjoys watching cartoons, including "Family Guy," "Batman," "Dragon Ball Z" and "Tom and Jerry."
- Often drinks coffee during position meetings.
- Likes to sneak up behind friends and spook them.
- Known as a daydreamer.
- Is a devout Christian.
- Parents Eugene and Darlene are both ministers.
- Expecting to graduate with a sociology degree at the end of the academic year.
- Joined teammates working with children this summer at Michigan GEAR UP/ College Day Program.

Source: The State News

Ringer's 1,112 yards on the ground and 14 touchdowns are both tops in the nation, making him arguably the best collegiate running back in the country.

The astronomical statistics aren't novel for the senior; in his three years as a starting running back at Chaminade-Julienne, Ringer averaged more than 2,000 yards and 25 touchdowns per season, despite missing half of his senior year with a torn anterior cruciate ligament.

As a runner, Ringer has all the gifts necessary to play on Sundays. He rumbles downhill like an out-of-control boulder, isn't afraid to deliver a devastating shoulder into a linebacker, has tremendous hands out of the backfield and loves to throw a crucial block for his quarterback.

"I see him a lot like a Willie Parker or a Clinton Portis type of back," said former MSU running back Jehuu Caulcrick, referencing the veteran rushers for the Pittsburgh Steelers and Washington Redskins, respectively.

Ringer's biggest question mark entering his senior season — his durability after tearing two ligaments in his right knee in three years — has been answered thus far. Despite carrying the ball more times per game than in Pee Wee, middle school, high school and his first three years at MSU, Ringer has emerged unscathed so far this season, proving his mettle for the NFL.

The adult
At 21 years old, Ringer has the maturity and loyalty of a man three times his age.

Ringer's education started early under his parents, Eugene and Darlene, both ordained ministers.

Once Ringer started gaining attention for his football ability (a 251-yard, four-touchdown performance for Chaminade-Julienne in Ohio's 2002 Division II championship game as a sophomore solidified his title as a football dynamo), he remained humble even as colleges started calling.

When recruiters from Ohio State, which Ringer first considered for college, started pursuing him, Ringer only listened to one school at a time.

"Picking schools is like dating a girl — you're loyal to whoever you're with," Ringer would tell his high school football coach, Jim Place.

Because his ACT score didn't meet Ohio State's academic standards, Ringer started focusing on the Spartans.

"The day (Ohio State's recruitment) fell apart, he said, 'No problem, coach. That's not God's plan for me,'" Place said.

During his recruitment by the Spartans, an assistant at Southern California, the Roman Empire of modern college football, called Ringer to ask if he would be willing to talk to Trojans head coach Pete Carroll. Ringer declined the offer because he wouldn't cheat on MSU's coaches.

After committing to MSU, reaching academic eligibility and emerging as one of the country's most explosive backs, Ringer maintained his low-key attitude.

Unlike the nation's bankers, Ringer takes all of his credit (which there is plenty of) and gives it away to everybody. Offensive linemen, fullbacks, tight ends, coaches and waterboys — each is more deserving of kudos than the ball carrier in Ringer's eyes.

And don't even get him started on the Heisman Trophy. He's more concerned about this week's game against Ohio State, whom he has never beaten as a Spartan. And next week, he'll spurn the bronze statute to focus on the Maize and Blue, which he also hasn't beaten. And the week after that, the Badgers will be in his sights. And the week after that ... well, you get the picture.

"I know he isn't sincerely thinking about it, but it would just be so awesome if he could win the Heisman Trophy and be a role model for all the kids out there," Place said.

Off the field, Ringer has never met an autograph he won't sign, a picture he won't take or a smile he couldn't make.

Whether it's speaking to young students about growing up, attending charity fundraisers or operating the inflatable bounce castle at elementary school carnivals, Ringer is one of the first MSU athletes to volunteer for community service.

When a group of elementary schoolers visited practice last week, many

Javon Ringer (23) attempts to pull away from the Fighting Irish in MSU's 23-7 win in 2008. Ringer finished with 201 rushing yards and two touchdowns. Sam Ruiz/The State News

wearing green Ringer jerseys, he crouched down and gave a wide grin, as if taking a school portrait in third grade, for each child wanting a photograph.

"As soon as I saw out there all the little No. 23 jerseys, I wanted to make sure I spoke to them and took some pictures with them just to make sure they come away here with a positive outlook on things and just a smile," Ringer said.

The adolescent

Ringer also is like those elementary schoolers waiting to meet their Spartan hero.

Hidden beneath his fierce running style lies a little boy at heart.

During Friday nights on the road last season, Ringer and Caulcrick, his roommate, could be found in their hotel room, watching professional wrestling. To carry over the previous night's lessons, the pair would wrestle over the remote Saturday morning when Caulcrick wanted to watch college football pregame shows and Ringer clamored for cartoons.

Like any youngster captivated by "Batman," "Dragon Ball Z" or "Tom and Jerry" cartoons (all favorites of Ringer's), he boasts a gullible side easily persuaded by authority.

In his younger days as a Spartan, older running backs would mischievously send Ringer to see coaches, like a middle schooler being sent to the principal's office, when he wasn't being summoned. Other times, players would usher Ringer onto the field during practice when his name hadn't been called.

In position meetings, Ringer is known as a daydreamer always in need of a cup of coffee. Although Enos said Ringer's lapses rarely last more than a minute and don't affect his performance, Caulcrick would later hear about his fellow running back's mental drifts.

"Man, do you ever wish you had Dragon Ball Z powers?'" he would ask Caulcrick, drawing a quick, "No, not really," in response.

Ringer's hijinks extend beyond the football team to the MSU athletics department's student-athlete support services.

Angela Howard, associate director of student-athlete development for MSU, who often seeks out Ringer for community appearances, has fallen victim to the senior's habit of trying to spook friends.

Ringer will sneak up behind Howard and others to scare them, which always draws a laugh from the Heisman Trophy candidate.

"I can't believe how many times he can get me," Howard said. "I keep telling him when he goes down on injured reserve because if I turn around and hurt him, it's not going to look good."

On the field, Ringer's laid-back personality helps carry him to record-setting numbers. Whether it's sitting on the bench cracking inside jokes or ribbing quarterback Brian Hoyer about his sack-saving blocks, Ringer's attitude doesn't waver.

"That's another reason why it makes him so special," Enos said.

Making sense of Ringer

So what drives a determined football player as playful as Dennis the Menace and humble as Mother Teresa to become a future NFL running back?

How do you make sense of Ringer, a rare breed of athlete who gets hit every week, wakes up early in the morning to lift weights but still makes everyone he meets instantly fall for him like MSU rushing records this year?

"Honestly, my number-one motivation is my family," Ringer said.

"I want to continue to work hard and be successful, so, Lord willing, I can go to the NFL and just be able to support my family.

"And two, I just love playing with my friends. It's fun being out here. People who don't actually play football, I don't know if they understand how it is just being out here with your brothers and the brotherhood that you develop being on a team. It's fun."

For the athlete in Ringer, it's about ending his senior season of college on a winning note, beating rivals he has yet to slay.

For the adult, it's about providing for family and honoring God by using his talents in the NFL.

For the adolescent, it's about playing with friends and having fun on a cool autumn evening, like any other child tossing around a football in his Dayton backyard. ∎

Javon Ringer (23) and sophomore wide receiver Mark Dell (2) greet the fans from the student section at Spartan Stadium after MSU's 2008 Homecoming victory over Iowa, 16-13. Ringer ran for 91 yards in the game. Katie Rausch/The State News

Time To Remove 'Same Old Spartans' Label

By Jacob Carpenter • November 1, 2008

The saying goes that those who don't learn from history are doomed to repeat it.

The 2008 MSU football team appears to have studied up and learned its lesson from last year after pulling out another close game with its 25-24 last-minute victory over Wisconsin.

With kicker Brett Swenson's 44-yard boot in the final seconds of Saturday's game, the Spartans officially relinquished the title of "Same Old Spartans." Where past teams would find a way to lose a close game (all six of MSU's 2007 losses were by a touchdown or less), the dogged Spartans are now snatching victory from the jaws of defeat.

Ignore the 250-plus yard advantage for the Badgers on the ground. Or the beating MSU's front seven took on defense. Or the 11-point Wisconsin advantage with less than 10 minutes to play. Or the 34 dropped passes.

What matters is the final score: Michigan State 25, Wisconsin 24.

When the MSU defense was called upon to make a late stop to give the Spartans' offense a chance to respond, they answered (with a little help from the referees) by squashing a 9-play Wisconsin drive and forcing a punt with less than two minutes to play.

When senior quarterback Brian Hoyer was asked to engineer a one-minute drill and lead his team 50 yards into field goal range, he pulled out his post-Halloween John Elway costume and completed three passes for 56 yards. And that was with two dropped passes along the way.

Finally, when Swenson, MSU's steady junior kicker, fresh off three failed field goal attempts last week, had a team's New Year's Day bowl hopes placed on his leg, he swung hard and straight for one of the best kicks of his career.

These Spartans are a new breed, one that has done their homework by limiting mental errors, making clutch plays in key situations and finding ways to win.

They are the Same Old Spartans no more.

That's a history lesson that would rather soon be forgotten than learned again. ∎

Above: Junior kicker Brett Swenson (14) looks to the sky after making his second field goal of the game against Wisconsin. Swenson made four field goals including the game-winner, defeating the Badgers 25-24. Sam Ruiz/The State News Opposite: Spartan fans cheer the players after their last minute win over Wisconsin. Nichole Hoerner/ The State News

Senior quarterback Kirk Cousins, center, and head coach Mark Dantonio, right, lead the Spartans into Spartan Stadium prior to their 2011 game against Youngstown State. The Spartans defeated the Penguins, 28-6. Josh Radtke/The State News

Leader Of Men

In a rare opportunity, the MSU football team has tapped a sophomore to lead the Spartans in battle

By Matt Bishop • October 15, 2009

Don Cousins came to campus a few weeks ago to hear his son, Kirk, speak to the members of Campus Crusade for Christ. MSU's sophomore quarterback held up the team's playbook for the team's well-documented rivalry game — the annual tilt with Michigan.

"He said, 'This is what the coaches have put together for the Michigan game and if we execute what's in this book, the belief is we can beat Michigan,'" Don recalled his son telling the group.

Then Kirk went on to tell of one playbook that never leaves his backpack.

"He held up the Bible and said, 'This is the playbook for life,'" Don said. "For me, as a dad, that little analogy right there summarized what my wife and I have been trying to be about with our kids since they were born."

Raised as a devout Christian by his parents, Kirk Cousins took the values and convictions he learned growing up in Chicago and Holland, Mich., and applied them to his life — as a son, student, friend and football player.

And although Cousins has five starts at quarterback for the Spartans this season and likely many more in his future, he won't allow football to define him.

Faith and family come first for one of MSU's most mature 21-year-olds.

Faith

One of three children, Kirk Cousins has been immersed in faith his entire life. He calls his father — who is in the ministry, speaks around the country and authors books that sell in Christian bookstores — "the major leader" in his life.

Cousins views his faith as a relationship with God — not making it a religion or about rituals, but a relationship.

"I want to talk to him, I want to be in prayer with him, I want to be giving him my requests and my worries and my stresses and the pressures I face," he said. "I want to give that over to him because he says, 'Cast your burdens on me because I care for you.' So he cares for me."

Before Cousins came to MSU in summer 2007, he was fresh off a two-week Bible study in Israel, a trip he said "really got me focused on what was most important right before I came here."

Raised in a Christian home and going to

Holland Christian High School, coming to MSU would be an enlightening experience.

"When I came to Michigan State, obviously it's a worldly place; things are very different," Cousins said. "People don't talk the way I'm used to hearing people talk back in Holland. People don't act the way I'm used to people acting back in Holland on Friday nights and Saturday nights, so I knew pretty quickly that if I wanted to honor the Lord, it was going to be more of a challenge

here than it was back at home. I was going to be more swimming upstream, going against the grain. I just checked myself right away. I said, 'Am I going to be a man and step up?'"

But it was a conversation with his father that really set the tone for him.

"He said, 'Kirk, we've raised you for 18 years now and we're letting you go. We have to figure out if you're going to be a man on your own or are you going to stoop to people's lower expectations or are you going to take the high road?' and I decided that's not going to be me," Cousins said. "I'm going to be somebody who takes the high road. That's what I did."

But being away from home weighed on Cousins early. He said he was homesick, scared and alone, despite his family being only 90 minutes away. He couldn't even imagine what his teammates from across the country — or students who came from across the world — were going through.

"I'm not a big person who likes change," he said. "But I just kept reminding myself that the Lord led me here and he's got a plan for my life and I'm going to trust him and trust that if I continue to honor him, he's going to have a plan and I can see now, two years later looking back, how the more I just stayed the course and just continued to honor him and not get sidetracked, he's continued to provide and honor me."

And that was important for Cousins to reaffirm his beliefs, considering what many students indulge in — partying, drinking, swearing — and the pressures of a major university's social scene.

"There's nothing wrong with going out, there's nothing wrong with having a couple of beers," he said. "Sometimes I may give people the wrong impression that that is wrong and I don't want to do that because there's nothing wrong with that."

Cousins said he's busy to the point that when he gets a chance to sit and watch TV, that's all he wants to do. After games, you can find him watching whatever football games are on at the time. He also is active in Athletes in Action and hosted a Bible study group for the team this summer, which 10 to 15 players regularly attended, he said.

Marching to his own beat

Don Cousins said he and his wife, MaryAnn, felt joy when Kirk was named a team captain in August — just the second sophomore captain in program history.

"Kirk has always been a young man who set the bar, so to speak," Don said. "He's always been someone who's marched to the beat of his own drum, as my wife likes to put it. He's an independent thinker and he has a strength of character that has allowed him really, over the course of much of his life, to make decisions for himself."

Don recalled a time Kirk was in high school and was invited to see a PG-13 movie with some friends. From a young age, Don said they always instilled the message, "When you make good decisions, good things happen, and when you make bad decisions, bad things happen," a simplified version of a proverb Don is fond of.

Don said Kirk researched the movie and it contained some questionable material, but Don let Kirk make the decision on his own, asking

him, "Would going to that movie be a good decision or a bad decision?"

Sure enough, Kirk called Don back a few minutes later and said he decided to pass on the movie.

"When something is unfolding that is not keeping with his own values and convictions, he has no problem with standing up and saying, 'I'm going to take a pass on that,'" Don said.

Cousins always has been ahead of the curve, always been a leader. Whether it's putting an arm around a teammate who fumbled or hanging out with members of the Spartan Marching Band on Sparty Watch, Cousins believes in doing the right thing.

"I want to have great success here as a student, as a football player and then as a leader on this campus," Cousins said. "I want to be a person who has some influence here on people, and students in general. I want to be a person that, when I leave, people say, 'He had a positive impact on this university.'"

Builder of people

Cousins isn't afraid to speak his mind in the locker room.

His speeches to the team aren't superficial — they have meaning, senior receiver Blair White said. Senior defensive end Trevor Anderson called them "powerful."

When Cousins was a senior point guard for the Holland Christian boy's basketball team, a freshman was brought up to varsity and likely would take a lot of playing time from two of Cousins' friends.

Sophomore quarterback Kirk Cousins scrambles from Western Michigan defenders at Spartan Stadium in 2009. Cousins would help the Spartans to a 49-14 victory with a career-high 353 passing yards on 22 completions. Sean Cook/The State News

"I looked down to the end of the court and I see Kirk standing around the free-throw line and he has his arm around this freshman kid," Don Cousins said, fighting back tears. "He's got his arm around this freshman kid and Kirk was clearly the leader of the team. ... For Kirk to put his arm around that kid before the game began was sending a message to that kid, as well as to his teammates, but specifically to that kid, that words can't explain. That's Kirk."

Running backs coach Dan Enos, who recruited Cousins to MSU while quarterbacks coach under John L. Smith, says the team really responds to Cousins' leadership.

"He's a guy that when he makes a mistake, he owns up to it," Enos said. "He never tries to point fingers at anybody else and actually probably puts too much blame on himself sometimes that he shouldn't, but that's what great leaders do."

Cousins said he leads by being positive and encouraging people, but he sometimes will get frustrated and have to "get in a guy's face a little bit."

"But I try to be somebody who builds into people and really invests in them," he said.

Cousins said a lot of leaders in America care about themselves more than others, and that's not the way to do things.

"What leadership is, is going down and bringing people up," Cousins said. "It's not, 'Look at me, I'm up here, come up to my level.' It's going down to their level and bringing them up and taking them to where they couldn't have gotten."

Anderson said he's watched Cousins blossom into the leader he is and, as a sophomore, Cousins has earned the right to say the things he does.

"He's not trying to overlead," Anderson said. "He's not letting people get in his head and tell him, 'Oh, you've got to do this and you've got to do that.' He's going out there and being able to play at the same time and knowing when to say something and when to shut up."

Don Cousins said Kirk understands what leadership is about — it's not all about being the hardest worker or the most diligent.

"My son understands leadership is about caring for his teammates as people," Don Cousins said. "He has lived that out in such a way that when they elected him as a captain, they saw that in him."

Enos said he "absolutely" would call Cousins a natural-born leader.

"I think that's a great way to put it," he said. "Some people can be great leaders and not be great players and some people can be great players and not be great leaders. We think he has the potential to do both."

Serious implications

Last October, Detroit sports personality and columnist Rob Parker said in a segment on WDIV-TV in Detroit that Cousins was involved in an off-campus fight that sent hockey defenseman A.J. Sturges to the hospital.

Cousins was with his family in their hotel room at the time. For anyone who knew Cousins, they likely knew the report was incorrect.

Cousins said the situation didn't bother him much because he knew he wasn't there.

Instead, his thoughts on the situation shifted to an unlikely source.

"Who I really felt bad for was the guy who wrote the story, because I thought he was the one who was going to take the hit on this," Cousins said.

Said Don Cousins: "I've got to admit, that wasn't the way I was looking at it."

MSU head coach Mark Dantonio came out at his weekly press conference two days later and defended Cousins.

"What's not fair to do is what Rob Parker ... from The Detroit News, who went on TV the other day, WDIV-TV Sunday night in Detroit and made a reference to Kirk Cousins being at the heart of this whole matter, which is totally inaccurate and I take offense to that, his family takes offense to that and he was with his family all night Saturday night and I think that borders on slander and if you're going to say something, you better get it right," Dantonio said.

"So, here's a young man who does everything right and he's thrown under the bus by somebody who has no credibility in my mind."

Don Cousins said Dantonio's aggressive defense of his son "meant a great deal" and the truth only affirmed who Kirk was.

Parker and the station later apologized to Cousins, his family and the university.

"Coach Dantonio has always done that, he's always defended our players and especially players who are trying to do the right thing all the time," Kirk Cousins said.

"We have a saying around here that, basically, what we say is, 'do the right thing all the time, period.' No matter what situation I'm

At the time Kirk Cousins ended his career at Michigan State he was the school's all-time leader in passing touchdowns (66), passing yards (9,131), completions (723) and passing efficiency (146.1 rating). He compiled a 27-12 record as a starter and his teams went 4-0 over Michigan. Kat Peterson/The State News

in, I'm going to try to do the right thing all the time. I think Coach D was just trying to defend a player who he trusted."

Self-proclaimed sinner

Through everything he does, Cousins is quick to point out he's not perfect.

When Cousins makes the rare off-color remark, his teammates are there to let him hear about it.

"Every now and then, a swear word will come out but they'll look at me and they'll catch me and say, 'Kirk, you can't do that. Not you.' And they almost coach me more than I coach myself making sure that I don't go down the wrong road," he said.

"I just tell them, 'Hey, that's Jesus Christ inside of me. That's not me. I'm a sinner. I'm a horrible person, but Jesus Christ inside is special and he can be special inside you, too, if you let him.'"

He says the team has been "great" about not ridiculing him for his strong faith and what he's trying to do.

And even if football doesn't work out for Cousins, he still has a bright future ahead of him.

On a premedical track, Cousins said it's his dream to play football as long as he can, but he's not counting on it.

He plans to put everything he has into football and school at MSU and "let the chips fall where they may."

He said he'd eventually like to go to medical school to become a doctor.

"It's truly rewarding to be here as a student and it's a real blessing to be here at this university and the support that we receive from the student body, the marching band and all that," he said.

"There's just such loyal fans here. It's just great to be a part of. I'm just living a dream, really, and hopefully there's better things in the future to come." ∎

Left: Cousins passes the ball against Montana State. He threw for 183 yards and three touchdowns in the 44-3 win over the Bobcats during the 2009 campaign. Angeli Wright/The State News Opposite: Kirk Cousins (8) runs the ball through the Penn State defense. The Spartans fell to the Nittany Lions 42-14 in 2009. Josh Radtke/The State News

Fake Field Goal Gives Spartans Overtime Win Vs. Notre Dame

By Jeff Kanan • September 19, 2010

All Aaron Bates did was react. As his team lined up for the potential game-tying field goal, the senior punter reacted normally to the big play call, reacted to the chasing defenders and threw an exceptional pass to senior tight end Charlie Gantt, who broke open, and finished the 29-yard touchdown play that gave MSU a 34-31 win over Notre Dame.

"I wasn't really thinking, I just kind of reacted," Bates said. "I just threw it and as soon as it left my hand, I was hoping that I didn't overthrow it."

The call, which was organized by Dantonio and the coaching staff, caught everyone in the stadium by surprise and came with the Spartans trailing by three in overtime.

Dantonio said he intended to run the play at some point Saturday, but the opportunity never arose until the Spartans were trying to attempt a 46-yard field goal trailing to tie the game.

He gave the play call to Bates, who accepted it casually, and watched it executed to precision, as did Fighting Irish head coach Brian Kelly, who was left shell-shocked.

"With a 47-yarder, I would have hated to have put that kind of pressure on (sophomore kicker Dan Conroy) and us come up short with it," Dantonio said. "He's very capable of it, obviously. The last kick of the game against ND, in overtime, to tie it. And I thought that we had a good chance to win. We had that play called 200 times (in practice) and we scored touchdowns."

It didn't go exactly the way it was intended to, as freshman running back Le'Veon Bell was expected to get the ball, but he inadvertently became a decoy when he ran into two Notre Dame players and let Gantt go free.

A former high school quarterback, Bates' pass was on target, and capped a game that saw the Spartans fight back never give up despite being in trouble late.

"Wow, what a football game," Dantonio said. "We executed. Gantt sneaks out there and gets separation and makes the catch. All of that doesn't work without execution."

The emotional scene at the end of the game was the exact opposite of last season's game against Notre Dame, when players hung their heads after junior quarterback Kirk Cousins threw an interception with time winding down in MSU's 33-30 loss.

It appeared headed for the same course Saturday with the Spartans trailing by a touchdown in the fourth quarter and Notre Dame's red-hot offense on the field in the fourth quarter.

But MSU's defense, which had surrendered touchdowns on Notre Dame's previous three drives and was being run ragged by the Fighting Irish's passing attack, rallied and forced a three-and-out and a turnover on Notre Dame's last two possessions of regulation to set up junior quarterback Kirk Cousins' 24-yard touchdown strike to junior wide receiver B.J. Cunningham to tie the game and eventually force overtime.

"This is a difficult loss, obviously," Kelly

MSU football players rush the student section after a thrilling 2010 victory against Notre Dame. A fake field goal turned into a touchdown pass to give them a 34-31 win.
Matt Radick/The State News

said. "It came down to one play, which MSU executed, and we did not. This was a game that went back-and-forth, it was a hard-fought game, but we came up short."

Bell led a stout MSU running game that accounted for 203 yards and followed up where it left off the two previous weeks.

He finished with 114 yards and a touchdown, but it was sophomore Edwin Baker's 56-yard touchdown early in the third quarter that went down as the most memorable.

After entering the locker room tied at 7-7 at halftime, the second half couldn't have been more unscripted.

Following Baker's touchdown run, Notre Dame responded with a 10-yard pass from Dayne Crist to tight end Kyle Rudolph to tie the game.

MSU answered with Bell's 16-yard touchdown run, before the Fighting Irish had an answer once again on Crist's pass to wide receiver Theo Riddick, who led Notre Dame with 128 yards receiving.

Notre Dame scored on quarterback Dayne Crist's 24-yard pass to Michael Floyd with 12:30 remaining in the game to take a 28-21 lead, but MSU responded with an improvised touchdown pass from Cousins to Cunningham with 7:43 to play.

Cousins finished 23-for-33 for 245 yards, two touchdowns and an interception.

Neither team converted on its final drives of regulation, and Notre Dame was held to a field goal on its first drive in overtime.

The fake field goal touchdown pass will go down as one more exciting finish in a rivalry that has seen plenty of them in the past decade.

"Like we said all along, we needed one big momentum play," Dantonio said. "We just didn't know when it would come. I don't really know where to start or to end. But it was a big night for the Spartans." ∎

Right: Freshman running back Le'Veon Bell breaks into the open field on his way to 114 rushing yards against Notre Dame. The Spartans out-rushed the Fighting Irish 203 yards to 92 in their 34-31 overtime victory. Matt Radick/The State News
Opposite: Social work junior Mike Grimaldi, left, and English junior Kevin Gorman react to MSU's unexpected and game-winning touchdown over Notre Dame. Kat Petersen/The State News

Dantonio OK After Heart Attack; Treadwell To Step In As Coach

By Jeremy Warnemuende • September 19, 2010

Football head coach Mark Dantonio will not be on the sidelines for Saturday's game against Northern Colorado after suffering a heart attack shortly after the Spartans' overtime victory over Notre Dame early Sunday morning.

Dantonio's return to coaching will be looked at on a week-by-week basis, said Dr. Chris D'Haem, an interventional cardiologist with Thoracic and Cardiovascular Institute at Lansing's Sparrow Hospital. The fourth-year MSU head coach is expected to spend several days in the hospital but make a full recovery from the heart attack, which he felt symptoms of at about 12:30 a.m. Sunday, after the game-winning fake field goal touchdown pass.

Dantonio's wife drove him to Sparrow Hospital's emergency room soon after, where he was treated immediately. D'Haem performed a cardiac procedure on Dantonio that restored blood flow to the heart muscle, according to a statement released by the MSU Athletics Department.

"He is young, in excellent shape, and the damage to his heart was minimal," D'Haem said in the statement. "Coach Dantonio made the right decision to come in and get checked out immediately."

While Dantonio is recovering, offensive coordinator Don Treadwell will manage the responsibilities of head coach, MSU Athletics Director Mark Hollis said during a press conference Sunday. Hollis said men's basketball head coach Tom Izzo assisted in deciding who would take over head coaching duties.

Treadwell said during the conference that he doesn't expect any issues maintaining the beliefs and philosophies Dantonio has instilled with the team because the Spartans have had the advantage of a lack of attrition among assistant coaches during Dantonio's tenure at MSU. The only coach to leave since 2007 was Dan Enos, who took the head coaching job at Central Michigan in January.

"Football-wise, certainly as (Hollis) mentioned, our thoughts go out to Coach Dantonio," Treadwell said at the press conference. "One of the things he has certainly done is he has put in place a tremendous program. There's been a model we've been following for four years here at Michigan State, three years previous to that (at Cincinnati). It lends itself to the fact that there's some great carryover that's already in place."

Treadwell said players were informed early Sunday afternoon of Dantonio's condition.

"I think they're handling it as well as they can," Treadwell said of the players' reaction to the news. "They love their head coach. We know that. It's our job as assistant coaches to keep them moving forward and focused on task."

Hollis, who said he visited Dantonio from 2:30 a.m. to 5 or 6 a.m. Sunday at Sparrow Hospital, asked that Dantonio does not receive any visitors while he rests at the hospital. However, Sparrow Hospital offers an e-card service through which messages can be left with patients. The service can be found under the online services tab at sparrow.org.

"He is our head coach (and) will remain our head coach throughout this whole process," Hollis said. "This is a time for the Spartan Nation to come together, to rally, not only for Coach Dantonio and his family, but in everything that we're doing here at Michigan State. ... We know Coach will return to the sidelines very soon." ■

Offensive coordinator Don Treadwell, who stepped in for head coach Mark Dantonio during Dantonio's health issues, walks off the field after MSU defeated Wisconsin 34-24 in 2010. Sam Mikalonis/The State News

Senior linebacker Greg Jones rallies teammate and fellow linebacker Steve Gardiner after a touchdown scored by wide receiver Mark Dell on Senior Day in 2010. Sam Mikalonis/The State News

Leaving A Legacy

Senior linebacker Greg Jones will play his final home game Saturday and go down as one of the best players in MSU history

By Jeremy Warnemuende • November 18, 2010

Greg Jones won't often be caught hesitating on the football field. Playing in all 49 games since he stepped foot on the MSU campus four years ago, Jones plays every snap to the whistle and seemingly at a higher level than everyone else around him.

However, on Sept. 1, 2007, when the Greg Jones era began in East Lansing, the then-freshman linebacker couldn't help but pause and take a break in the action — even if only for one second.

"The first time I ran on the field, I remember running like halfway through the tunnel, and I kind of stopped," Jones said. "I looked around, and it was either (linebacker Kaleb Thornhill), (safety Nehemiah Warrick) or one of the guys said, 'You got to keep moving.' And, I was like, 'Oh yeah, yeah.'"

Jones will take the field at Spartan Stadium on Saturday for the final time in his collegiate career. He might not have come to MSU very highly recruited, but he leaves as one of the best linebackers — and players — in school history.

Jones' journey to his first collegiate game wasn't a typical one, which is one of the reasons he made that initial entrance into Spartan Stadium last a little bit longer than it was supposed to.

Coming out of Archbishop Moeller High School in Cincinnati, Jones was a three-star recruit with only one Big Ten scholarship offer from Minnesota. Wanting to fulfill his goal of playing Big Ten football, he accepted the offer and was set to join the Golden Gophers in 2007.

But two months before National Signing Day, Minnesota head coach Glen Mason was fired, and everything changed. Jones opened up his recruitment, and fortunately for him, MSU head coach Mark Dantonio was about to become a Big Ten coach as Mason's days in the conference ended.

Dantonio, who recruited Jones when he was the head coach at Cincinnati, was hired as the Spartans' head coach in November 2006 and still had Jones on his radar. So when Jones became available, Dantonio went after him, eventually convincing Jones to come to East Lansing.

Four years later, nearing the end of what Dantonio calls a "tremendous career," Jones hasn't stopped for anybody since he had to be pushed out of the Spartan Stadium tunnel before his first game.

"I knew then I'd be hooked, and I have been ever since," Jones said. "I'm addicted to it. I love it."

Exceeding expectations

Jones is set to go down as one of the best linebackers ever to put on an MSU uniform.

Leading the Spartans in tackles each season he has been at MSU, twice he has been named to the All-Big Ten First team, and last season, he was selected as a First-Team All-American and the Big Ten Defensive Player of the Year.

But early in his career, Jones said he simply was hoping to get on the field.

"When I first came here, I told (linebackers coach Mike Tressel), 'I just want an opportunity,'" Jones said. "I remember talking to the special teams coach and just asking him a whole lot: 'Can I just get on the field and make a play?' That's all

I've ever asked for, just to prove myself."

With 446 tackles and 44.5 tackles for loss (both third in school history), Jones has proven himself and then some.

Although Dantonio said he thought Jones would be good when he first saw him play in high school, nobody expected him to do as much as he has during the last four years.

"I thought he'd have an outstanding career here based on his abilities and what I saw in camp when I was at (Cincinnati)," Dantonio said. "But you never really know if a guy will transition that to college football. He has."

Tressel has been Jones' position coach for all four years of his MSU career. After watching Jones capture nearly every award and honor a linebacker could win, he said he wouldn't expect a career like Jones' out of any recruit.

"You never assume that's going to happen with anybody," Tressel said. "Everybody you recruit, you hope and you see something that makes you think they're going to be really good. Certainly, we saw things with (Jones) we thought would make him be really good."

With Jones' coaches and even he himself somewhat surprised at what he's been able to accomplish as a college football player, seemingly the only person who saw it coming was Jones' father.

"Well, we knew all along what was going to happen because we could see it in him," Greg Jones Sr. said. "With his motivation and everything, we knew what the future was going to hold."

Jones Sr. introduced his son to football when he was about seven years old, and he said he knew, even back then, that the younger Jones would go on to do big things.

"He was successful at everything he had done — basketball, baseball, band and in the classroom," Jones Sr. said. "He was successful all along."

Finishing up

This Saturday, Jones will begin putting the finishing touches on his successful college career when he and the 16 other seniors play their final home game against Purdue.

With a win, Jones and the 2010 class can become the winningest group of seniors in MSU history with 32 victories. Jones said all the wins had less to do with him and more with the play of the whole team — a team he almost wasn't a part of this season.

After his junior campaign, Jones flirted with leaving for the NFL. But in January, Jones announced he was coming back, not only to improve his draft status for next year and to get his degree, but to win a Big Ten championship.

At 9-1 overall and 5-1 in the conference, the No. 11 Spartans still have a chance to do just that.

"My mom always said, 'There's a purpose, there's a reason why you came back,'" Jones said. "I firmly believe in that also, and I'm happy to be a part of it."

Along with the chance to compete for a conference crown and a potential trip to the Rose Bowl, Jones' return also means he gets to participate in Senior Day — a moment he said will be very important for him and his family.

"Enjoying Senior Day will be special, especially for my parents," Jones said. "Those two people have put in all the hard work — I feel like more than me. Just every day, starting from little league all the way up to high school and now."

When he is honored along with his parents on the field before Saturday's game, Jones said he doesn't know how emotional it will be. However, Jones said if his dad, who knew all along his son would be great, breaks down, he will too.

"That could happen," Jones Sr. said. "It will be his last home game of his career. It's a great moment for me and him and his mother. I think it may be emotional, but I'm looking forward to it."

As for the actual game, Jones hopes it goes much like his first game at Spartan Stadium, when he had seven tackles and a sack in a 55-18 win.

Although, he hopes the entrance goes a little more smoothly this time around.

"Hopefully nobody has to tell me to keep going," Jones said with a smile. "Other than that, I just want to have fun out there, but more importantly, try to get the win." ∎

Senior linebacker Greg Jones, along with several other football team members, made an appearance at a Michigan State basketball game to show off their new hardware, the

At Long Last

Spartans bring home Big Ten championship

By Jeremy Warnemuende • November 28, 2010

Nobody saw this coming four years ago. Fresh off a 4-8 season in 2006, during which MSU won only one Big Ten game, the Green and White faithful likely assumed the football program would be knocked down to Division II before it won a conference championship.

Those were the darkest days of the "Same Old Spartans," and it appeared MSU was in a hole it never would be able to climb out of.

But four years later, here we are.

Four years after John L. Smith was run out of town and Mark Dantonio was brought into East Lansing as the new head coach, the No. 7 Spartans (11-1 overall, 7-1 Big Ten) have a share in the Big Ten championship for the first time since 1990.

And nobody saw it coming. Well, almost nobody.

Senior linebacker Greg Jones became the gem of Dantonio's first recruiting class. And although he was committing to a program with three straight losing seasons and no promise of moving up at the time, Jones had a feeling things soon would be different.

"The culture change started back when I was recruited," Jones said. "The first thing (Dantonio) talked about was winning, and what it was going to be like. Now, we don't find ways to lose, and people have to realize this is a different Michigan State."

If "Little Giants," "Mousetrap" and a third straight win over rival Michigan didn't clue people in to the fact this isn't your daddy's MSU football team, then the Spartans bringing the Big Ten hardware back to East Lansing should do the trick.

Especially considering the way they did it.

Jones, who passed on the NFL after last season to come back and win a conference championship, had it exactly right: MSU teams of years past would have found a way to lose to Penn State on Saturday in State College, Pa.

With the Spartans ahead 28-10 midway through the fourth quarter Saturday, MSU almost did just that. The Nittany Lions scored two quick touchdowns, and with a minute to go, Spartans everywhere were having horrible flashbacks of Braylon Edwards plucking passes away from undersized corners and coaches slapping themselves in the face. However, after MSU made a few head-scratching mistakes to let Penn State cut the lead to 28-22, the Spartans did just enough to win in Happy Valley for the first time since 1965.

"We can't do it the easy way, can we?" junior quarterback Kirk Cousins joked after the game.

Nope. But in a season like the one the

With seconds left in the game, head coach Mark Dantonio smiles as confetti falls around him in celebration of the Spartans' win over Penn State, 28-22, which earned MSU the Big Ten Championship for only the seventh time in school history. It was also the first time since 1965 that MSU beat Penn State on their home field, Beaver Stadium. Kat Peterson/The State News

Spartans just finished, it only was fitting that they kept things interesting.

Because nothing about 2010 was easy.

There were plenty of opportunities for MSU to find ways to lose all year long. Whether it was in overtime against Notre Dame, after falling behind early in games to Purdue and Northwestern or committing three first-half turnovers against No. 4 Wisconsin, the Spartans could have thrown it all away on more than one occasion.

But was Dantonio — who oh, by the way, missed two games following a heart attack suffered right after the Notre Dame win — worried about anything?

He wasn't worried about MSU becoming a winner when the program was a Big Ten bottom-dweller, why start when it had a chance to win a championship?

"There was no concern on my part when I came here in '07, that we'd be successful," Dantonio said. "It was just a matter of time."

Turns out that matter of time was four years, and now the Spartans are getting fitted for Big Ten championship rings.

It didn't happen right away. It started with three straight bowl appearances, which Dantonio called building a "foundation."

Now, the foundation of the MSU football program is stronger than it's been in a long time, and Dantonio has done more than simply build a winner.

He, along with Jones and all of the other seniors who have helped change the perception of MSU football, has built a champion.

So the next time the Spartans squeak out close games they have no business winning, fight through all of the adversity thrown at them and win another championship, maybe more people will see it coming. ■

Right: Kirk Cousins holds the game ball after the Big Ten Championship-clinching victory over Penn State. Cousins finished with 152 yards passing and two touchdowns. Kat Petersen/The State News Opposite: Head coach Mark Dantonio directs his team to come to the sidelines during the Spartans historic win over Penn State. Matt Hallowell/The State News

A Hail Of A Win

Spartans clinch penalty-free win over Badgers, 37-31, with last-minute 'Rocket'

By Michelle Martinelli • October 23, 2011

As senior quarterback Kirk Cousins heaved the ball 44 yards up the field on a Hail Mary pass, senior wide receiver Keith Nichol waited patiently to see where it would fall.

Nichol ran up the field and stopped a couple yards short of the end zone — where senior wide receiver B.J. Cunningham and sophomore tight end Dion Sims already were waiting. The ball slipped through Wisconsin wide receiver Jared Abbrederis' hands, bounced off Cunningham's face mask and popped back up toward Nichol.

After Nichol's catch was ruled a touchdown, Spartan Stadium erupted in celebration of the game-winning play. Nichol was in the right place at the right time.

"'There's no way I didn't get in on that' — that's the first thing I thought," Nichol said after MSU's 37-31.

"We just call that 'Rocket.' Every team has that play."

From starting his college career as a true freshman quarterback at Oklahoma, Nichol said he never would have imagined he'd become a developed wide receiver who won the game for MSU on a tipped ball.

"We talk about (how) you don't know when your time is going to come for you to make a play," head coach Mark Dantonio said. "You have to believe that you're going to be the guy that makes the play because you don't know when you're going to have that opportunity."

In what Dantonio and players called a team effort, the Spartans quickly fell down 14-0 early and used a safety, two interceptions, a blocked field goal and a blocked punt to take down Wisconsin.

But while Nichol, Cunningham and senior wide receiver Keshawn Martin were on the receiving end of big plays, it was Cousins' arm making the difference.

With Saturday marking his 22nd career victory, Cousins now is the winningest quarterback in MSU history. In his 20th career 200-yard game, he completed 22-of-31 passes for 290 yards and three touchdowns while outplaying Heisman hopeful Wisconsin quarterback Russell Wilson.

Pleased with his performance, Dantonio said Cousins was "on the money" Saturday — not only in his down-field throw to Nichol, but also in his numerous completions to Martin and Cunningham, including a fourth-and-two 35-yard touchdown pass and a two-point conversion.

"I have nothing but great things to say about him," Cunningham said. "We all have had his back the whole time, and I feel like he came out (Saturday), led us to victory, and he deserves

Senior wide receiver Keith Nichol catches a tipped ball for the touchdown for the dramatic win over the Badgers. The Spartans defeated Wisconsin 37-31 on Kirk Cousins' Hail Mary pass to Nichol. Josh Radtke/The State News

to be the most winningest quarterback here, and I wouldn't want anybody else to have it."

Despite Cousins receiving some criticism this season, senior offensive guard Joel Foreman said Cousins is "a blessing to have" on the team because of his ability to lead the Spartans out of a two-touchdown deficit to finish with a game-winning, 44-yard "rocket" to the end zone.

"It's a testament not to me, but a testament to my teammates and a testament to the program that our coaching staff has built," Cousins said.

"I don't think many people gave me a chance coming out of Holland Christian (High School) to be anywhere close to the winningest quarterback here."

MSU rose to the occasion on national TV when many people — including College GameDay's Lee Corso — picked the Spartans to lose a big game such as Saturday's. When the team responds by controlling the game to take the win, junior defensive tackle Jerel Worthy said the team grows closer together.

Continuing to win games that the Spartans are predicted to lose shows what kind of team and program Dantonio is developing, Worthy said. Coming from behind, Dantonio trains his players to fight until the end, and it paid off this time around.

"Week in and week out, nobody (ever) really wants to give the Spartans a chance," Worthy said.

"We've just kind of got to go out there and keep playing with a chip on our shoulders. To be honest, I like being the underdog because you really have nothing to lose."

"Everybody is picking against you anyway, so when you go out there and shock the world, it feels great." ∎

Right: Senior wide receiver B.J. Cunningham runs for a touchdown against Wisconsin
Opposite: Mark Dantonio and offensive line coach Mark Staten hug after the emotional win over the Badgers. Josh Radtke/The State News

Junior running back Le'Veon Bell smiles as he walks toward the center of the field after defeating Boise State 17-13. Bell rushed for 210 yards and two touchdowns in the 2012 home opener. Matt Hallowell/The State News

Bell Gains National Spotlight With Strong Showing Against Boise State

By Jesse O'Brien • September 4, 2012

After his 265 total-yard, two-touchdown performance against then-No. 24 Boise State Friday night, junior running back Le'Veon Bell has been thrust into the national spotlight, raking in Offensive Big Ten Co-Player of the week honors and eliciting talks of possible Heisman candidacy.

However, head coach Mark Dantonio doesn't want the accolades to get to Bell's head.

"I think what we have to make sure [we don't] drink the Kool-Aid around here," he said. "He's always tried to be a complete football player, so I don't think that's going to change whether he's blocking or catching the ball or running with the football. I think he would play on special teams if we asked him to, and I think that's the trademark of a good player.

"So his attitude is in the right place right now."

While Bell's statistics are staggering, they also came at a heavy price. The 6-foot-2, 244-pound running back touched the ball 50 times on the night, including a personal-high 44 carries.

"I had no idea (I would get that many touches," Bell said. "(Offensive coordinator Dan) Roushar just told me be ready to carry the ball. I was expecting about 20 to 25 touches but they needed me in the third and fourth quarter more times than not, and I just made sure I was ready for it."

With a very inexperienced passing game in junior quarterback Andrew Maxwell and his receiving corps which consists of one junior, four sophomores and one redshirt freshman, Roushar has turned to Bell to shoulder most of the load on offense. However, the unit's heavy reliance on Bell calls into question how much his body can take over the course of a 12-to-14 game season.

Bell said the load was intense, but one he could handle for the good of the team.

"I was sore (the next day)," he said. "When I got out of bed I felt real sluggish. I didn't want to move. But once I got into the weight room and started lifting and running, I got my body back and my legs back under me."

However unlikely it might be, if Bell were to continue being fed the ball 44 times a game, he would record 528 carries during the regular season, shattering the previous program high number of 419 set by Lorenzo White in 1985.

Still, Dantonio said he doesn't see reducing the junior's carries any time soon.

"(We'll run him) until he gets a flat (tire), I guess," he said. "He was hot. I've said many times here we're going to ride the hot back."

And as far as senior running back Larry Caper sees it, there's no reason not to continue giving Bell the opportunity to take it down the field.

"Everyone has their limit," Caper said. "But if (Bell) continues to get 50 touches a game and continues to show durability, keep giving him his touches and he'll keep producing."

500

90 years of Green and White: Spartan Stadium will host its 500th game Saturday

By Matt Sheehan • October 10, 2013

Spartan Stadium isn't just a building.

Buildings don't give hundreds of thousands of fans memories to talk about when they drive out of East Lansing on fall Saturday nights.

Buildings don't bring former head coach George Perles back to the emotional stories of the journey to the 1987 Rose Bowl.

Buildings wouldn't bring the hearty laugh of TJ Duckett as he recounts the hard days of summer practice on the hot turf.

Spartan Stadium isn't just a building — it's a landmark.

Born in 1923 with a plot of grass and a set of 14,000 wooden bleachers, the Michigan Agricultural College, or MAC, Aggies logged their first season on a field with no name.

Three hundred and thirty-six home wins, 30 All-Americans and six national titles later, the grounds of Spartan Stadium will host its 500th game tomorrow. It will be the 500th time roaring fans and the men in green and white will be creating memories that could last a lifetime.

"Just talking about it right now, I am getting goose bumps," former running back Jehuu Caulcrick, who played with the NFL's Buffalo Bills in 2010 said when talking of Domata Peko's 74-yard defensive touchdown against Michigan in 2005.

That was loudest Caulcrick ever heard the stadium roar, with the energy of years of construction, remodeling and the passionate fans all coming undone in the moment.

Cherished memories

Nearly a decade before he strapped on the green Spartan helmet, former running back TJ Duckett walked into Spartan Stadium with wide eyes. Watching his brother, former running back Tico Duckett, who wore the green and white 1989-92, and a sea of green pour out of the stadium's tunnel, the memories of TJ Duckett's would-be stomping grounds started when he was 9 years old.

"When I was just a kid, (the stadium) was huge," TJ Duckett said. "Seeing the big guys run out of the tunnel, seeing the band, seeing the student section, and seeing the alumni, it really looked like (the) Colosseum with the gladiators."

With the fans raised so high off the playing field, Duckett observed the stadium looks like the Roman Colosseum with the fans looking down at the battle between the lines.

One of 12-year head coach George Perles' fondest memories came from being barreled over by overzealous fans in 1987, after the Spartans clinched a Rose Bowl bid with a 27-3 win over Indiana.

Spartan Stadium was built in 1923 with 14,000 wooden bleachers. After the most recent expansion in 2005, the stadium capacity is up to 75,005 and has been home to countless memories along the way. Natalie Kolb/The State News

"That is when we had the 3-foot wall from the stands," Perles said. "I got knocked down and I got trampled by everyone, and someone picked me up and that was the most chaotic it has ever been."

That somebody was his defensive line coach, Steve Furness. Without Furness preventing his coach from being run over, Perles might not have witnessed one of his favorite Spartan Stadium memories.

"I was talking to the team (after the win), and Indiana's coach (Bill Mallory) busted in and motivated our guys said how we will beat USC," Perles said.

And they did. The Spartans took the 1988 Rose Bowl trophy back to East Lansing after defeating the Trojans, 20-17.

But the locker room held more memories than emotional pep talks and post-game celebrations. Caulcrick still gets chills on the back of his neck whenever he remembers the dramatic pre-game routine leading up to kickoff.

"After you warm up, you go into (the locker room) and there is that five-minute period where everyone is silent getting their mind right for the game," the running back from 2004-07 said. "All of the sudden the band starts playing in the tunnel, and the locker room walls start shaking, and that's when you know it's time to go."

For TJ Duckett, however, his favorite recollections are months before making the first run out of the tunnel during the first week of football season. With the summer sun heating up, the artificial turf – which was ripped up in 2002 and replaced with grass – gave off a distinct smell he still recognizes today.

"Your brothers (were) out there, training when the stadium is empty with nobody watching what we are doing," the former seven-year NFL player said. "Guys' characters were tested, wills were broken and champions were made right there, and those are personal moments people don't see."

Right: The football team walks on the field prior to their 21-6 victory over South Florida in 2013. Julia Nagy/The State News Opposite: Spartan Stadium lights up the MSU campus on Aug. 26, 2012. The new scoreboards in both the north and south end zones were unveiled days later on Aug. 31, as the Spartans topped Boise State 17-13. Adam Toolin/The State News

The hallowed grounds

Where Old College Field now lays the MAC Aggies, the nickname prior to "Spartans," played their earliest football games. In 1924, MAC football changed forever with a $160,000 state grant — more than $2 million in 2013, adjusted for inflation. The location was a decision George Blaha, radio play-by-play voice of nearly four decades, still believes to be the best part of Spartan Stadium.

"The best thing about Spartan Stadium is that it is right in the middle of one of the most beautiful campuses in America," Blaha said.

The biggest feature the stadium was missing until 1935 was an official name, when it was branded as Macklin Field and the seating capacity was raised to 26,000.

Roughly a decade later, the stadium saw its most drastic change in 1948 when the university nearly doubled the capacity, creating a total of 51,000 concrete-reinforced seats. With MSU football coming into the public eye and enrollment boosting by nearly 5,000 between 1948 and 1956, the seating was increased to 60,000.

One year later, the upper decks were erected on both sides of the stadium, but not without an immense amount of stress coming from administration. In a memorandum from the Office of the Secretary of MSU to the American Bridge Company, the builders of the decks, a slight sense of panic arose as deadline drew near.

"Tickets will have been sold for all the space in the upper deck. It would be a calamity of major importance and untold embarrassment to the University if anything should happen so that the Stadium is not completed by (Sept. 28)," Secretary Karl H. McDonel wrote.

$2.5 million and an untold amount of patience later, the upper decks were completed before the season started. The next big change wasn't for the bleachers — it was for the playing surface, when MSU opted to ditch the natural grass field for artificial turf in 1969. Vice President for Administration and Public Affairs Jack Breslin calculated it would cost $15,000 to resod the turf every five weeks, thus the decision to spend $250,000 on a field built by Tartan Turf.

After three decades of playing on the soft synthetic turf, MSU made the switch back to natural grass, naming professor of turfgrass management Trey Rogers to oversee the project. For Rogers and many others in the turfgrass program, it was a move that made sense.

"(Implementing grass) was something that for probably for 15 years we were working behind the scenes," Rogers said. "When you have a turf program that is so highly thought of around the world, especially when you have (artificial) turf in your own backyard, we got a lot of questions from people, especially around the '90s."

It was a decade later when U2 came in for a concert during the summer of 2012,

setting steel plates all over the field during the course of setting up for and performing the concert. Unfortunately for Rogers, the grass he, professors, graduate and undergraduate students grew died from lack of sunlight and had to be removed.

In 2012, with the help of Rogers selecting the right farm to replace the grass, Graff's Turf Farms in Fort Morgan, Colo,. sent 26 refrigerated trucks filled with sod to Spartan Stadium to give the field fans look at today.

"The Spartans have the best grass field in America," Blaha said. "(Sports Turf Manager) Amy Fouty was in charge of that, and she needs to be congratulated more than she is."

2005 saw the priciest stadium transformation — $64 million — with the construction of new suites, press boxes and a new facade on the west end of Spartan Stadium. Caulcrick, who played through the stadium transformation, said he noticed the decibels grew as the tall tower kept the crowd noise on the field.

"You go to Michigan and you're at the Big House, but realistically that place is not loud because they pack the people in like sardines (and) the sound escapes," Caulcrick said. "That is why we get a louder crowd at Spartan Stadium." ∎

Spartan Stadium was alive during a rare Friday night game, featuring new scoreboards and a triumph over No. 24 Boise State. James Ristau/The State News

Run This State

Behind the strength of a record-breaking defense, MSU lands biggest win over U-M since '67

By Dillon Davis • November 3, 2013

During Saturday's game against Michigan, MSU paid tribute to Percy Snow.

One of the most talented linebackers in program history, and the leader of MSU's 1987 Gang Green defense, Snow became notorious for his nose for the backfield, earning him the Butkus and Lombardi awards, a Rose Bowl victory and eventually, a spot in the College Football Hall of Fame.

Few were more feared; few were more integral to their team's success.

Yet, a greater honor to one of college football's hardest-hitting linebackers came in the game with the Wolverines, as the No. 18 Spartans physically punished Michigan quarterback Devin Gardner all afternoon, totaling seven sacks and holding U-M to -48 yards rushing in a 29-6 win at Spartan Stadium.

The win marks the largest margin of victory for an MSU team against U-M since 1967, and the defense held Michigan to the fewest rushing yards in a single game in the history of the program.

Contributing two sacks in the game, senior linebacker Denicos Allen said the defense felt the tension of the Michigan offense each possession and big play.

"We definitely felt the frustration coming from them," said Allen, who was named the Walter Camp Football Foundation national defensive player of the week for his efforts. "Every time (Devin) Gardner would get hit he would kind of get up with this look of frustration and kind of doubt."

Sophomore quarterback Connor Cook threw for 252 yards with one touchdown and one interception, along with a fourth quarter rushing touchdown that sent Cook fist pumping down the sidelines and junior center Travis Jackson jumping up and down at the goal line.

Cook's lone touchdown pass was to senior wide receiver Bennie Fowler, who pulled down the fade pass in the corner of the end zone for his fifth receiving touchdown of the season.

Fowler was MSU's leading receiver of the day, finishing with six receptions for 75 yards and a touchdown.

And while the overwhelming defensive output is not lost on anyone, Cook said the Spartans stayed poised on the offensive side of the ball, feeding off the energy of the defense to score points when given the chance.

"We continue to say that as an offense that we go against them every single day, we've gone against them for the past however many years and we do good against them," Cook said. "So if we do good against them, we can do good against

Michigan State players celebrate with the Paul Bunyan Trophy after the Spartans' win over the Wolverines in 2013. The Spartans' 29-6 win was their biggest over the Wolverines since 1967. Khoa Nguyen/The State News

any defense in the country, and I think that's what we did today."

Early in the game, the teams struggled to move the football through sloppy playing conditions, trading field goals until MSU's final offensive drive of the first half, which was capped by Fowler's touchdown reception to put the Spartans ahead, 13-6.

Another field goal by freshman kicker Michael Geiger made it a two-possession game with his third quarter 35-yard field goal.

The game could have turned after Cook threw an interception near the end of the third quarter, giving the Wolverines a fighting chance in a matchup of Big Ten heavyweights.

But the defense held Gardner from taking a shot at the end zone, forcing him to lose five yards on the next play from scrimmage followed by back-to-back sacks to give MSU the ball back in the fourth quarter.

From there, Cook added seven points with a one-yard rushing touchdown, while junior running back Jeremy Langford capped the day with a 40-yard touchdown run to send Spartan Stadium into a state of jubilation.

"Our crowd came to play today," head coach Mark Dantonio said after the game. "They had their game face on from the get-go. I thought they were passionate. They were excited, and it was deafening down there."

Right: Jeremy Langford rushed for 120 yards in Michigan State's 2013 win over Michigan. Julia Nagy/The State News Opposite: MSU head coach Mark Dantonio exchanges handshakes with Michigan's Brady Hoke after the game. Khoa Nguyen/The State News

However, the talk of the team remains the defense, who thoroughly bullied the Wolverines in an effort reminiscent of MSU's 2011 victory over U-M.

"It feels good, anytime you can press the quarterback like we did," senior linebacker Max Bullough said. "You talk about how it was a physical beatdown out here ... And that is a complete game for us."

Heading into a bye week, the Spartans now turn their sights to Nebraska, who likely will be the last team standing between MSU and a Big Ten Legends Division title and a trip to the Big Ten Championship Game on Dec. 7.

Closing the book on another MSU win against Michigan — the fifth in seven attempts during the Dantonio era — Dantonio said the Spartans take great pride in the program with plenty to look forward to in the coming weeks.

"I can just tell you that we do what we do," Dantonio said. "There are guys that they have on their football team that we haven't offered, let's get that straight right now. There are guys on our football team that they've never offered, so it's what you do with the players that come and what their belief system is. Our guys are believing."

And for Bullough, the goal remains the same as it ever was.

"You know this will last the rest of my life," Bullough said. "But we have a few more games left — and the Rose Bowl, that's gonna last the rest of my life." ∎

Right: Linebacker Denicos Allen tackles Michigan quarterback Devin Gardner during the game. Opposite: Safety Kurtis Drummond celebrates after an incomplete Michigan pass falls out of bounds. The Wolverines' quarterbacks completed just 15 of 30 passes. Danyelle Morrow/The State News

A Deeper Look At 'Charlie Brown'

Fake field goal call was key to Spartans' 41-28 win over Nebraska

By Stephen Brooks • November 18, 2013

If everything went according to plan, MSU's fourth-quarter fake field goal — code name: Charlie Brown — would not have happened.

"I was excited to run it because every time we ran it in practice I ended up scoring a touchdown," junior punter Mike Sadler said.

"But the look that they gave us was different, and I was actually supposed to check out of that and we were supposed to kick a field goal."

Sadler didn't notice the different alignment at the time, and went ahead with the fake instead of a 45-yard field goal attempt from freshman kicker Michael Geiger.

The situation required additional ad-libbing after the snap. Sadler said Charlie Brown is designed to be an outside run to the right (MSU also has "Lucy" in its playbook, the same play going to the left) but the hole was clogged so he turned it inside to grind out three yards and a first down.

An attempt at deception turned into a power run for the 192-pound punter with Geiger assuming the role of lead-blocker through the teeth of the defense.

So did Geiger throw a good block up the middle?

"I have no idea. I'm just gonna go ahead and assume no," Sadler said. "I'll have to watch film. I just remember being picked up ... I'm just glad that I lived to see another day."

Head coach Mark Dantonio has established a reputation for special teams trickery, and Sadler's run Saturday setup a Connor Cook touchdown pass that put the Spartans in control the rest of the way.

Sadler has become something of a secret weapon for MSU, rushing for 25 and 26 yards on fake punts at Iowa this season (that one was coined "Hey Diddle Diddle Send Sadler Up the Middle") and at Michigan in 2012.

"At some point in time your head football coach has got to take chances," Dantonio said. "That's the basic thing. I told our football team at halftime, hey, we're gonna roll the dice, and that's what we were gonna do. I'd already made up my mind on that series if we got within field goal range than we were running the fake — Charlie Brown."

Cook said he was confident in the call considering the team's success rate when running it in practice, and noted Sadler has "one of the strongest bench presses" on the team.

"He's a really, really strong guy. Doesn't really look like it, but he's a lot stronger than you think," Cook said. "... Anytime the ball's in his hands I feel comfortable, I feel like he's gonna protect it and if he has to lower his shoulder, he's gonna."

"What was it? Fourth-and-1 or fourth-and-2? I figured we could at least get that with Sadler running the ball up the middle," senior linebacker Max Bullough added. ∎

Punter Mike Sadler runs the ball during a fake field goal attempt against Nebraska in 2013. The fake punt, known as Charlie Brown, was a key play in the Spartans' 41-28 in over the Cornhuskers. Khoa Nguyen/The State News

Kyler Elsworth Seals MSU's Rose Bowl Victory Over Stanford

By Stephen Brooks • January 1, 2014

PASADENA, CALIF — Before the game it was about the middle linebacker. After the game it was about the middle linebacker.

When senior Max Bullough's career was pronounced dead via an email in the wee hours of Dec. 26, it jolted the MSU community eagerly readying itself for the biggest game in more than two decades. His departure stole the headlines from a team looking to prove it belonged among the nation's best.

It was former walk-on Kyler Elsworth, a career backup with a knack for making big plays, who filled Bullough's void as the starting middle linebacker in the final game of his career.

Elsworth, the unlikeliest of heroes as a fill-in for an accomplished defense, sealed a 24-20 win for the fourth-ranked Spartans against No. 5 Stanford in the 100th Rose Bowl with his late-game aerial tackle on Cardinal fullback Ryan Hewitt on fourth-and-1.

"I said I've got one chance here, I've got to go over the top because they're taking out legs on the D-line so I ended up going up top and ... I made a big play," said Elsworth, who was named defensive MVP, as confetti precipitated through the cool California air.

"I couldn't be happier."

Elsworth's Superman-esque stuff gave the ball back to the Spartans with 1:43 left on the clock while Stanford was out of timeouts. Three quarterback kneels — with senior Andrew Maxwell taking the final snap — kicked off a celebration 26 years in the making.

MSU ended its longest Rose Bowl drought since its maiden voyage to Pasadena, Calif., in 1954 with a win and improved its record to 4-1 in the legendary game.

The Spartans lost the first quarter, but won the final three in front of an amped-up crowd of more than 95,000, most of which was draped in green.

After ceding 146 yards in the first 15 minutes, MSU's vaunted defense clamped down on the Cardinal attack and allowed just 159 during the next three quarters.

"You win with toughness," head coach Mark Dantonio said. "There's no question about that. You win with toughness, physically and mentally, and I thought we did that tonight."

Stanford scored a touchdown on the opening drive of the game, knocking the vaunted Spartan defense on its heels.

A busted coverage from sophomore cornerback Trae Waynes on the second play from scrimmage allowed for a 43-yard bomb from Cardinal quarterback Kevin Hogan to receiver Michael Rector. That play paved the way for a rumbling 16-yard touchdown from standout running back Tyler Gaffney.

After a Stanford field goal made it 10-0, sophomore quarterback Connor Cook led a 13-play, 75-yard drive for his team's first touchdown: a 2-yard sprint by junior running back Jeremy Langford.

Cook made some poor decisions, resulting in one interception returned for a touchdown

Head coach Mark Dantonio and quarterback Connor Cook hold the Rose Bowl trophy following MSU's 24-20 win over Stanford on January 1, 2014. The win marked the Spartans' first in the Rose Bowl since 1988. Julia Nagy/The State News

and two more passes that Stanford easily should have grabbed, but he finished with a career-high 332 passing yards and two touchdowns. He claimed offensive MVP honors after being named MVP of the Big Ten Championship Game.

Ironically, Cook's pick-six was the turning point for MSU.

The Spartan offense trotted onto the field with slightly more than two minutes separating them from halftime and remained aggressive rather than melting the clock. Cook delivered a big throw to junior Tony Lippett for 24 yards and an arcing lob to senior Bennie Fowler to Stanford's 3-yard line. The chunk plays setup a 2-yard touchdown reception by sophomore fullback Trevon Pendleton to cut the deficit to three by halftime.

MSU tied the game at 17 on the first possession of the third quarter off the leg of freshman kicker Michael Geiger from 31 yards out.

Lippett took a post route 25 yards to the house, dragging a defender with him to the end zone, to give the Spartans their first lead, 24-17, early in the fourth quarter. MSU took advantage of a short field after a 19-yard punt return by sophomore receiver Macgarrett Kings Jr. started its drive on Stanford's 27-yard line.

The Cardinal faced a third-and-16 from the MSU 28 after senior defensive end Denzel Drone dropped Hogan for an 8-yard sack on the previous play and had to settle for a 39-yard field goal after failing to convert the first down.

Stanford was on its own 34 when Elsworth's decisive leaping stop put the game away in a play that will live on in Spartan lore for years to come. He wasn't truly alone, though, as sophomore linebacker Darien Harris, who split time at linebacker with Elsworth, and sophomore defensive end Shilique Calhoun got a piece of Hewitt as well.

Right: Thousands of Spartans fans from across the country traveled to Pasadena to watch the game, including MSU alumni Drew Yamanishi (left) and Bo Torres. Opposite: The bruising MSU defense takes down Stanford running back Tyler Gaffney. Julia Nagy/The State News.

"You have to give it to Michigan State for stuffing that because everybody in the building knew exactly what was coming, a run was coming up the middle," Gaffney said, "and it was a test of wills, and they got the better of us."

Elsworth, a former standout wrestler who at one point was unsure if he would pursue a football career, made the most of his only career start.

"It was under circumstances that were unfortunate, but the coaches trusted that in me to step in and (do) the job just like Max has done for years now," he said.

"It means a lot to me coming from a walk-on, working my way up the chain, (I've) been in every situation to have the coaches have faith in me, it means the world."

MSU concludes the season with 13 wins and now has a three-game bowl winning streak — both feats are school records. The Spartans are assured a top-five spot in the final rankings.

More importantly, the players were adamant the Rose Bowl victory was a perception-altering game on a nationally televised stage.

"We should be (considered) elite. We're top five. Anytime you talk about college football, Michigan State should be named," cornerback Darqueze Dennard said after ending his decorated Spartan career. ■

Right: A Spartans fan looks on during the 125th Rose Bowl Parade. Opposite: Fans enter the stadium for the 100th Rose Bowl game between Michigan State and Stanford. Julia Nagy/The State News

Keep Your Enemies Close

MSU—U-M rivalry goes beyond football, influences relationships

By Emily Jenks • October 23, 2014

"**BEAT** Michigan" shirts. Smack talk on social media. U-M's block 'M' spray-painted green with "S-U" scrawled next to it.

A taxidermied wolverine in a maize and blue vest, hanging by a noose from the back of a van with license plate "ST8 VAN" along with a banner reading, "The only good Wolverine ..." parked outside the Starbucks on Grand River Avenue.

There's no mistaking it — it's Michigan week.

But even with all the animosity, harsh words and pranks from both sides, many MSU students have family, friends and even significant others behind enemy lines.

House divided

International relations junior Ali Bazzi and his sister Amani Bazzi, a U-M student, have more than just a sibling rivalry.

Ali Bazzi said they grew up U-M fans wearing maize and blue gear as little kids since their dad was a fan, but Ali Bazzi chose to attend MSU instead.

"Now (my dad) is a die-hard Spartan since I went to MSU," he said. "He switches it up every day, really."

His father got them an MSU–U-M "house divided" flag, which they posed with outside their home in Dearborn Heights.

Ali Bazzi and Amani Bazzi's younger siblings, a freshman in high school and an elementary student, have already shown preferences in the green-and-blue family.

"My high school sister is a die-hard Michigan fan and my little brother is 9 and is always talking crap about Michigan and wearing State gear," Ali Bazzi said. "My sister (Amani Bazzi) will always tell me Michigan is better, but even she knows that they're probably going to lose this year."

A rough beginning

As Dantonio and athletic director Mark Hollis are prone to say, Michigan residents are either green or blue.

Spartans' competitiveness is so intrinsic to the university that the original "Michigan State Fight Song" said, "smash right through that line

of blue/watch the points keep growing," instead of "go right through for MSU." Also, "see their team is weakening" was once "Michigan is weakening."

The rivalry between U-M and MSU is not just about a football game. The rivalry's roots go back to MSU's beginning in 1855 as an agricultural school that U-M wanted for their own.

There has been bad blood between the institutions since U-M failed on their 1837 promise to create a competent agriculture program. Agricultural College of the State of Michigan, MSU's original name, was created in 1855 instead.

U-M tried several times to stop the Agricultural College of the State of Michigan from forming and over the next several years. U-M then tried to absorb the agricultural college as it grew and expanded its programs.

However, alumnus Jeff Hicks said he thinks the true sports rivalry began long after the agricultural battle.

"I think it's been a rivalry ever since U-M voted to keep Michigan State from joining the Big Ten. I think that's what started that level of

Senior running back Jeremy Langford goes down at the one yard line on Oct. 25, 2014, during the game against Michigan at Spartan Stadium. The Spartans defeated the Wolverines, 35-11. Julia Nagy/The State News

friendly animosity," he said.

Hicks is part of a Spartan legacy. His grandmother graduated from MSU in the '20s, his mother in the '60s, himself in the '90s and he has two nieces who attend MSU today.

"For those of us that grow up with (the rivalry), and have lived through it ... our whole lives ... it means that much more," he said.

It's complicated

Elementary education sophomore Laura Krieber and U-M student Carter Lee began dating when Krieber was a freshman at MSU and Lee was still deciding where to attend college.

"I remember when I kind (of) went after him. I said, 'you should come to Michigan State, it's awesome,'" she said.

Little did Krieber know that Lee's father graduated from U-M's dental school and his heart had been set on U-M since he was a little kid.

The pair decided to give their romance a try despite going to rival schools. At tailgates and family events, each refuses to wear the other school's colors.

Despite having a healthy perspective on the rivalry, Krieber said she does wish they went to the same school.

Krieber and Lee both said they were glad the rivalry gave them something to joke about, and Krieber said she bonds with Lee's family in a strange way due to their rivalry.

"I'll wear Michigan State shirts on purpose over to his house," Krieber said. "If Carter comes here (for tailgating) and is wearing Michigan, I wouldn't associate with him," she said with a laugh.

Lee said the rivalry hasn't put any strain on the relationship, but it does add excitement to it, despite U-M's lacking football program.

"We're having a little bit of a sub-par year. Hopefully we can pull off a little bit of an upset, but hopes aren't too high," he said.

Family ties

Computer engineering sophomore Matt Boboltz and his father, Scott Boboltz are both Spartans, but his older brother and sister are U-M graduates.

"My sister went into English, and my brother went into language. So I think in that respect U-M might have been a better choice for them. We're from Okemos as well, and they didn't really want to stick around," Matt Boboltz said.

Scott Boboltz said when his kids first decided to go to U-M, there was an initial moment of disappointment.

"At first it was a momentary letdown or whatever. ... But U-M, aside from the sports, is an outstanding school," he said. "Come game day, I'm totally green."

Scott Boboltz said U-M is still a dangerous team and called the game a "pure rivalry."

"As far as the disdain between students, I think it's all in fun at the end of the day," he said. "At least, I hope it is."

Judi Cottrell is a U-M alumna with a daughter at MSU, media and information senior Nicole Cottrell.

"They (my kids) were raised right, she just chose to go to a different school," Judi Cottrell said.

Judi Cottrell said she has baby pictures of Nicole Cottrell in U-M onesies.

"Yeah, that was kind of weird for her to

support MSU. My philosophy was if you graduate and get a job it'll be fine," she said.

She said since her daughter Nicole is in the Spartan Marching Band, she'll go to MSU tailgates — but will wear maize and blue socks with her "MSU mom" sweatshirt.

Big trophy, little brother

It's no secret that MSU's football team is heavily favored against U-M this year. But that doesn't change the air of excitement and anticipation that takes hold of Spartans during Michigan week.

It's also no secret that the University of Michigan has, historically, not taken the rivalry as seriously. U-M student Lauren Haber said MSU is not a top priority for the maize and blue.

"I think if you're an in-state student you consider (MSU) more of a rival, but overall I think we have bigger and better schools to worry about, definitely Ohio State or Notre Dame," she said.

U-M's team is currently 3-4, and 1-2 in the Big Ten. They were shut out by Notre Dame for the first time since a 1985 game against Iowa. Their 2014 season was the first time in the program's history it lost every game in September. Last year, MSU held U-M to minus 48 rushing yards.

But it's no secret that U-M students, alumni and fans like to remember the past.

The Paul Bunyan-Governor of Michigan Trophy was introduced as a rivalry trophy in 1953 when MSU joined the Big Ten against U-M's wishes. In 1954, when U-M won the Paul Bunyan-Governor of Michigan Trophy, it was reportedly left on the field for a half hour before someone thought to go get it. The 4-foot tall trophy and its 5-foot tall base were left in a U-M locker room for the next two years and the university refused to engrave the scores for the '54 and '55 games, according to MSU University Archives & Historical Collections.

In 1956 it was reclaimed by MSU, which engraved the scores for U-M's two wins, in addition to their own, and put it on display in Jenison Field House. The trophy stands there today, awaiting the outcome of Saturday's matchup.

The first time U-M was reported to have celebrated winning the trophy was after a late-game comeback resulted in a Wolverine win in 2007. Then-running back Mike Hart coined the infamous "little brother" remark.

"I thought it was funny. They got excited. It's good. Sometimes you get your little brother excited when you're playing basketball and you let him get the lead. Then you come back and take it from him," Hart said in his infamous comment.

Head coach Mark Dantonio seemed to predict MSU's following success when responding to Hart's comments, reminding Michigan, "Pride comes before the fall."

And some might say Hart doomed his successors — after the "Little Brother" game, MSU won four games against U-M in a row, meaning none of the graduating seniors in 2011 won a game against MSU.

In the past
Over the course of the 116-year and 106-game rivalry, both programs have had periods of domination.

In 1902, U-M destroyed State Agricultural

College, as MSU was called at the time, in a disturbing 119-0 blowout. From 1916 to 1933 the agricultural college managed only 15 points against the Wolverines. U-M also enjoyed long win streaks in the '40s, '70s, '80s and early 2000s.

Michigan leads the series 68-33-5 all-time, 35-24-2 since MSU officially joined the Big Ten in 1949.

But MSU has not sat quietly. Since Mark Dantonio took control of the program in 2007, MSU has lost only twice to their cross-state rivals.

MSU Alumni Association president Scott Westerman graduated in 1978 in the middle of an era dominated by U-M and said he thinks the tides have turned.

"If you look at where the University of Michigan is now, they've had a lot of transition too in their program, so they're trying to rebuild, just like we were trying to rebuild back then," he said.

Westerman said he believes Dantonio's recruiting process and consistency has solidified MSU's dominance.

"It's almost like we are sitting in the seat that Michigan was sitting in back when I was here, and it's a pretty good seat to be sitting in," he said.

New traditions
Despite the intense feelings on both sides, Westerman said that the rivalry is a "one plus one equals four relationship."

"Each of us bring our own strengths to the table and we need a strong University of Michigan and a strong Michigan State University within the state. The state is better because we have two strong institutions here," he said.

Westerman's wife, Colleen Westerman, was treated at the University of Michigan Comprehensive Cancer Center with cisplatin, a drug developed at MSU.

Westerman said he believes the MSU–U-M rivalry shouldn't be about tearing each other down, but about what the universities can do together to attack the world's problems.

That isn't to say, of course, that Westerman isn't competitive.

"Do I want to win? Yeah! I want to win on Saturday. I want it to be a slam dunk victory too, but I don't hate Michigan," he said.

Westerman said he is excited for a new tradition — Alex's Great State Race. ROTC members from MSU and U-M will run the game ball from Michigan Stadium in Ann Arbor to Spartan Stadium in eight-mile increments. One ultramarathoner will run the entire 64 miles.

The race is inspired by the life of Alex Powell, a Lansing Catholic High School graduate who found out his senior year he had a rare and deadly form of cancer.

Despite this setback, Powell wanted to be a Spartan. The MSU Resource Center for Persons with Disabilities made that possible, but Powell passed away his freshman year.

His parents were so impressed by the RCPD, Westerman said, that they created the new tradition to raise funds for the center and U-M's counterpart.

"It is symbolic for us of the path that our two great schools have taken, to become as wonderful as they really are, and also the accessibility that is the hallmark of what Michigan State University is all about," he said. ∎

Iron Man

Senior defensive end Marcus Rush will see his 49th career start on Saturday against Ohio State, matching the MSU record

By Robert Bondy • November 4, 2014

For all of his career, senior defensive end Marcus Rush has lived in the shadows of the guy opposite of him. Whether it be five star All-American recruit William Gholston or NFL first round projection junior defensive end Shilique Calhoun, Rush has always flew under the radar earning the title "silent but deadly" by one teammate.

Regardless of not receiving as much attention from national and local media as his teammates, Rush has built a resume at MSU that some would consider untouchable. This week against No. 13 Ohio State, Rush will match the record for most career starts in MSU history, helping the Spartans become a household name during the process.

Mix in Rush's ties to the state of Ohio, and Saturday serves as an impactful day for the iron man of MSU football.

Evolving over time

Not many current Spartans can say they saw substantial playing time as a freshman, especially on the defensive side of the ball.

Rush not only has been a regular name in the starting lineup, but a regular force on the field for MSU. During his career in green and white, Rush has been selected to multiple freshman All-American teams, All-Big Ten teams and is once again making noise this season.

The Cincinnati, Ohio native was recently selected by ESPN and Phil Steele for its Midseason All-Big Ten second team with stats already nearly better than last season. Through the first eight games, Rush is only two tackles shy of last year's number with 28 already this season. He also has recorded 6.5 tackles for loss, 3.5 sacks and one forced fumble this season.

Since his first start back in 2011, Rush said he has been able to continue to learn more about the game, ultimately leading to his latest success now as a fifth-year senior.

"Freshman year, you're new to the whole experience, you're really focusing on trying to learn where you're going, what you're supposed to be doing, how you're supposed to be acting and trying to learn the plays," Rush said. "As you get older you start learning the system, everything just comes second nature and that's really when you start playing better because you're playing faster."

Rush's progression over the years not only has played a role on his current ability on the field, but also on the improvement of his teammates.

Multiple players talked about the impact Rush has had on the progression of his defensive teammates, but none have been more affected than his defensive end partner — junior Shilique Calhoun.

Through the past two seasons, Calhoun has received a lot of national attention as one of the

Marcus Rush shakes hands with junior snapper Taybor Pepper before Michigan State's game against Michigan on October 25, 2014. When Rush started against Ohio State on November 8, 2014, the fifth-year senior matched the Michigan State record for career starts. Erin Hampton/The State News

best defensive ends in the country, even recently being named a semifinalist for the 2014 Chuck Bednarik Award for most outstanding defensive player. However, Calhoun doesn't take all the credit for his success, pointing to Rush as a primary reason for why he's received his national accolades and recognition.

Calhoun said he was watching Rush on film as recently as last week, and considers learning from Rush's tendencies and past experiences as a key factor in molding himself into the player he is today.

"I've watched him since my freshman year on campus and he's been someone I've tried to model my game after," Calhoun said. "He's definitely someone I've watched over the years and I've been thankful to be on the same team as him because he's taught me a lot."

Record setter
Over the last four years MSU's defense has seen the likes of Spartan legends Max Bullough, Darqueze Dennard, Jerel Worthy and Denicos Allen but none have seen more playing time than Rush.

This Saturday against Ohio State, Rush will etch his name into the Spartan record books with what will be his 49th career start. The game will match the record for most career starts at MSU with former linebacker Eric Gordon and offensive lineman Joel Foreman, with only one more start in the final few games giving Rush the record all to himself.

Rush has been part of the Spartan starting lineup since his redshirt freshman season, appearing in four rivalry games against Michigan, two Big Ten Championship Games and three bowl game victories, including last year's Rose Bowl.

When looking at the record, Rush said all of the starts came through hard work and being able to gain the trust from his coaches to keep him on the field throughout his career.

"It's definitely an accomplishment," Rush said. "It just kind of comes with the hard work and the toughness and making sure I'm doing my job each week. If I'm not doing my job or the coaches aren't liking what I'm doing, obviously I wouldn't be getting those starts so just that in itself. Just making sure I'm staying consistent."

Rush added that staying healthy has played an obvious role in staying on the field.

Junior outside linebacker Darien Harris said at the beginning of the season head coach Mark Dantonio talked about the record with players as something to look forward to. On Tuesday, Dantonio said Rush's contribution during his time at MSU has been substantial, especially in big games like this upcoming week's matchup against the Buckeyes.

"He's a heart and soul type of guy," Dantonio said. "Extremely tough guy, plays very well, plays with his hands very well, is a playmaker on the field, made a lot of plays for us throughout the years and in big games he has risen up and played extremely well."

Silent leader?
Even from before he was sporting green and white on Saturdays, those close to Rush said he never needed to be the "life of the party."

During Rush's time at Archbishop Moeller High School, John Rodenberg served as his head coach for his junior and senior seasons, and considered it a treat to coach Rush. Rodenberg said Rush was always a quiet guy but served as a leader through his actions on and off the field.

"It was kind of funny because he was a fun guy to be around but he wasn't that class clown or didn't need to be the life of the party," Rodenberg said. "He was just a guy who commands so much respect because you see him in the weight room and see what he does on the field and that really attracts a lot of people to him."

While Rush is known as a quiet guy when it comes to talking to the media, that isn't always the case when he is in the locker room.

Harris has been Rush's neighbor in the locker room since he came to MSU, and said the side of Rush fans get to see isn't the same way he acts around the team.

Harris said Rush never brings a bad mood into the locker room and helps relax the guys through jokes and his upbeat attitude toward the game of football.

"He's a really fun guy to be around, never in a bad mood," Harris said. "Always a cheery guy, always makes jokes so he's really not that quiet around us which is really good because you need leaders like that to be outspoken and he's definitely one of the top leaders on this team."

Playing for respect
Saturday's matchup against Ohio State already has added significance, but any time Rush goes up

against the Buckeyes, it becomes personal.

Rush was heavily recruited by a number of Big Ten schools during his process, earning scholarship offers from Michigan, Nebraska and Purdue among many others. But Ohio State never showed much interest in the three-star defensive end recruit.

Rodenberg said during the recruiting process Rush never received a lot of attention from the Buckeyes because he wasn't the prototypical size for a defensive end that Ohio State was looking for at the time.

"They stayed away from him," Rodenberg said. "Ohio State wanted the biggest defensive end as they could get and I'm sure that turned him off from Ohio State."

Combined with growing up in the state of Ohio, this week serves as one of Rush's most anticipated games of the year. Rush holds a 2-1 record against the Buckeyes and said he always gets excited when the Scarlet and Gray are next up on the schedule.

"For myself especially, being an Ohioan it's definitely something more special," Rush said. "Whenever this game comes up in the week I'm extremely excited." ■

Defensive end Marcus Rush tries to push past Michigan offensive lineman Mason Cole during the Spartans' 2014 win over the Wolverines. Julia Nagy/The State News

MSU Comes Back To Win The Cotton Bowl, 'Never Lost Belief'

By Geoff Preston • January 1, 2015

ARLINGTON, TEXAS – The clock read 4:03 remaining in the third quarter when 390 pound lineman LaQuan McGowan scored on an 18 yard touchdown reception to give Baylor a 41-21 lead in the 79th Goodyear Cotton Bowl Classic.

That was enough for MSU. They decided to do something about it.

21 unanswered points ensued, including the go-ahead touchdown with 17 seconds left on a 10-yard pass from junior quarterback Connor Cook to senior wide receiver Keith Mumphery. After that, all that was left was the confetti.

"I really can't put it into words," head coach Mark Dantonio said. "We knew they had a good football team. And when they made a play, we regrouped and kept trying to play."

It was the largest bowl comeback under Mark Dantonio.

"It's fitting," senior punter Mike Sadler said. "We found a way to claw back, there is just not a better group than these guys."

It may have been fitting but it wasn't always pretty. MSU gave up 603 yards passing which included scoring plays of 49, 53 and 74 yards. Connor Cook threw two interceptions, one of which could have cost the Spartans the game because it killed a momentum building drive in the fourth quarter.

Despite that, senior safety Kurtis Drummond said everyone remained positive on the sideline.

"You know it was funny," he said. "You just kind of felt the vibe around the team remain positive, people were still jumping up and down and dancing, we just never let ourselves get down."

The Comeback

Players had a hard time agreeing on which play sparked the comeback, but they all agree at some point the momentum changed, and it changed in favor of MSU.

"I think it was probably the kickoff," senior defensive end Marcus Rush said. After a touchdown made it 41-28 Dantonio put decided to go for a surprise onside kick that MSU recovered.

"Even though we didn't score on that drive," Rush said. "I think that's when things started going our way."

Senior wide receiver Tony Lippett said it was hard right after the fact to point to a moment, but he said the blocked field goal was probably what sparked the team.

"I don't really know," he said. "But I do know that return by R.J. was great, it set us up."

With less than two minutes to play Baylor lined up for a 43 yard field goal that would have put Baylor up 44-35, and probably would have put the game out of reach. What happened was a blocked field goal that was recovered by R.J. Williamson, setting up what would be the game winning drive.

The adversity

Before the pass from Cook with 17 seconds left fell into the hands of Mumphrey, the game looked to be well in Baylor's hands.

Senior running back Nick Hill looks up to the AT&T Stadium ceiling after kissing the Cotton Bowl trophy following Michigan State's thrilling win over Baylor.
Erin Hampton/The State News

The first four possessions were track meets, MSU used balance while Baylor scored quickly and before everyone could find their seats the game was tied at 14.

After that, Baylor looked like a team the College Football Playoff committee missed out on.

"They had some big plays on us," he said. "But they're a timing team. You're going to play with your back to the ball a lot the way they throw the ball, so nobody has really stopped them."

Baylor threw for 603 yards on MSU, with 550 coming from senior Bryce Petty, which is a new Cotton Bowl record.

"(It's hard) to appreciate it because we lost," he said. "Not to be a jerk, but it's all for naught when you lose."

When MSU did get some of the momentum back after recovering an onside kick, Cook threw and ugly interception in the red zone that seemed to give Baylor the game again.

Cook struggled during portions of the game, finishing 24-42 with 314 yards, two touchdowns and two interceptions, but remained calm on the final drive.

"Obviously I would have liked to have played a little better," Cook said. "But it's not about how you start, it's about how you finish. It sounds cliché, but it really is."

MSU has now had to come back in their last four bowl wins against Georgia, TCU, Stanford and Baylor. Last season Cook had to bounce back after throwing a pick six in the Rose Bowl to lead the comeback against Stanford.

"I never lost belief," he said. "I never doubted myself or our team."

Right: Connor Cook celebrates after Keith Mumphery's fourth quarter touchdown catch gave the Spartans a 42-41 lead. Opposite: Cook looks to pass against Baylor. The Spartans quarterback threw for 314 yards and two touchdowns in the Cotton Bowl. Erin Hampton/The State News

The future

The moment many people latched onto after the game was an image of defensive coordinator Pat Narduzzi and Dantonio sharing a tearful embrace after the win. Narduzzi is leaving following this game to become head coach at Pittsburgh.

"You want the best for your people," Dantonio said. "To win the last game like that for coach Narduzzi was something that will be a memory for life."

Narduzzi said he was able to keep is emotions in check, until Dantonio asked him to have a special moment when he was recognized during the final practice.

"During the last practice all of the seniors go down and shake everyone's hands," he said. "That was great until coach said go down there and say goodbye to the seniors, but it was a great way to say goodbye to my players."

As with a lot of programs, the juniors are expected to fill the void when the seniors leave, after the game both the seniors and the juniors said that is their expectation for next season is for that tradition to continue.

"It's up to the juniors on this team to take the program to the next step," junior linebacker Darien Harris said. "We've already been history-makers here like coach said and set some records, now it's time for us to take this program to the next level."

For some, the future does not consist of football, or that future is clouded by uncertainty. Senior defensive end Marcus Rush said all the emotions that come with a comeback win in the Cotton Bowl and football potentially being over hasn't hit him yet.

"It's probably not going to hit until I get back home," he said. "I'm just trying to enjoy it right now." ∎

Right: Receiver Tony Lippett runs past the Baylor defense. Lippett led all Spartans receivers with five catches. Opposite: The Spartans and Bears practice on the AT&T Stadium Field before the Cotton Bowl. Erin Hampton/The State News

MSU Football Program Sets High Goals For Upcoming Season

During the team's first practice and media event, key players and coaches discussed the team's new motto, "Reach Higher," and what it means for the Spartans

By Matthew Argillander • August 12, 2015

Camp began last Saturday with a conditioning test everyone passed, including the freshmen in their first practices as Spartans.

"Well, we're in day three of practice, the first day of shells today, so I thought things went very, very well. (Everyone) paid a lot of attention, just getting ourselves back into football shape a little bit," head coach Mark Dantonio said at Football Media Day on Monday. "But today a little bit more active. Things speed up a little bit for everybody. Young players are taking strides."

Reaching higher

Despite their recent success, the Spartans are not satisfied. The approach to the summer, the training camps and the upcoming season has been the same — reach higher. That also just so happens to be the mantra for the 2015 season.

"We won 11 games, we ended up No. 5 in the country, we did what we did, but the fact of the matter is we lost two games ... if we win either of those games, I think we are a little farther along," Dantonio said. "We didn't succeed in those two games so we didn't reach our goals, and that's the bottom line."

Dantonio has built his team with a permanent chip on its shoulder. For a team that has every right to soak in the spotlight for a bit, there is no complacency or room for error.

"We've always come to work in winter workouts. We've always come to work in our bottom line program, summer camp, and I don't sense any complacency at all," Dantonio said. "I think our guys have goals in mind, goals internally, what they want to do, and I think right now in summer camp ... I think our guys are motivated on those. Now we need to be able to stay motivated, too."

This team is motivated by more than its championship goals. Being overlooked in the past still fuels the Spartans.

"A part of being fueled is the national championship, but we still look back on the past and understand that we have been overlooked," fifth-year senior defensive end Shilique Calhoun said. "We can always get back to a point where people say 'That's just Michigan State.' So that's our fuel, trying to not to be the perception of the old Michigan State."

The 2015 football team has 20 redshirt

Senior Connor Cook and teammates complete drills during Michigan State's first practice on August 8, 2015. Joshua Abraham/The State News

seniors. The leadership that comes with that leads to lofty goals. Teams normally shy away from stating their expectations verbally, but this MSU team has made their goals clear — playoffs or bust.

"A benchmark for us is going to be certainly getting to the playoffs and all those type of things, that's where our goals are," Dantonio said. "Our seniors because they're now into their last turn, their last three or four months here, and they understand, and I think the urgency of the situation, what has to happen and what they have to do to lead because that's been the nature here, I think, of what we've tried to do."

"We've had great senior leadership, and probably our seniors have always had their best years. When we've had big years, our seniors have had their best years, and that's a positive."

Boys of the summer

Despite not being able to work with the team for a majority of the summer, Dantonio knows his guys have been hard at work and it's shown in the first few days of camp.

"I think our players worked extremely hard in our bottom line program, which is, 'Hey, you're getting it done or not getting it done at the end of the day,'" Dantonio said. "Got a lot of players lifting a lot of heavy weight, a lot of players running extremely well. We look like we're in shape."

Redshirt senior linebacker Darien Harris believes the veterans on the team went the extra mile in workouts and preparations this summer to gear up for a season where the playoffs and a national championship are ultimately the goals.

"A lot of hard work (this summer), we know that the ultimate goal is to do better than we did last year, so we went into the summer hoping that we could do some things that we didn't do last summer. Going that

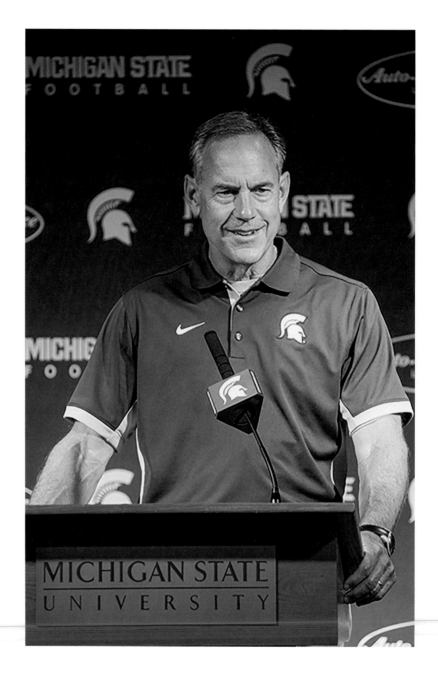

Right: Head coach Mark Dantonio addresses the media during MSU's media day on August 10, 2015. Catherine Ferland/The State News Opposite: Defensive line players take snaps during the team's first practice. Joshua Abraham/The State News

extra step, going that extra mile," Harris said. "Overall, it was a really good summer for us, the veterans, and when the freshmen came in they came in working hard, which we were really pleased to see."

It's that leadership from Calhoun, Harris and the other veterans that builds the foundation for success, according to Dantonio.

"I think the leadership has been very good early in this camp from our senior group, and that's always extremely important," Dantonio said. "I think there's great direction within our program at the ground level, which is, again, that's at the player level. When you have that at the player level, I think that gives you an added advantage, especially in games on the field because players lead on the field."

2014 first-team all-american and fifth-year senior Jack Allen stated that the team ran harder than they ever have before.

"All summer the o-line has been working hard, the whole team with 7-on-7s and drill work. We've been running a lot, I would say this summer we ran more than we have in past summers ... Wouldn't you say Don?" Allen said, looking for reassurance from teammate and senior offensive guard Donavon Clark .

Clark concurred.

This team won't be satisfied with past results and after a summer of hard work the Spartans will continue to put in the work to improve every day.

"If you look at our basketball program, I don't think Coach Izzo has ever been satisfied," Dantonio said. "I don't think (being satisfied) is the makeup of a coach or the program, or any real program, any championship-type program or program that's won a lot successively."

"We're going to come to work every day, that's all I can tell you. We're not going to take things for granted."

The first game of the season takes place on Sept. 4, when the Spartans travel to Kalamazoo. ∎

Right: Linebacker Riley Bullough takes questions during MSU's 2015 media day. Opposite: Defensive end Shilique Calhoun talks to members of the media. Catherine Ferland/The State News

MSU Football Team Makes Statement In 31-28 Victory Over Oregon

By Ryan Kryska • September 13, 2015

After the MSU football team's 31-28 win over Oregon on Saturday night, Dantonio said the experience of having previously played the Ducks and the home environment were worth three points – the margin of victory.

"I think last year was new territory for us," Dantonio said. "We were going to Oregon coming off of a Rose Bowl. Not a perfect game by any stretch, but we kept on playing."

In a game where the MSU defense allowed 432 yards, Dantonio said fourth down stops were keys in the victory.

"Come up with two big stops, one on the goal line and one at midfield. Really three big stops," Dantonio said.

Dantonio also praised the play of senior quarterback Connor Cook, senior wide receivers Aaron Burbridge and Macgarrett Kings Jr. and junior wide receiver R.J. Shelton.

Cook finished the game with 20 completions on 32 attempts, 192 passing yards, two touchdowns and one interception.

Burbridge had eight receptions for 101 yards and a touchdown and Kings had six receptions for 48 yards.

Above: Mark Dantonio looks on before MSU's game against Oregon on September 12, 2015. Joshua Abraham/The State News Opposite: Linebacker Chris Frey engages the Spartan Stadium crowd during the first quarter. Catherine Ferland/The State News

The key factor blind to statistics, however, was the play of the Spartans' offensive line. Cook had ample time to throw all game and was never sacked.

"The o-line played exceptional keeping me protected and making big holes for the running backs," Cook said.

Senior center Jack Allen was a major part of the offensive line's exceptional play. Allen said he had been thinking about what it would be like to walk off the field today with a with since Thursday.

"I would say this is probably one of the best feelings in the world," Allen said.

The running backs, redshirt-freshman Madre London and freshman L.J. Scott, combined for 179 yards rushing and Scott had two touchdowns.

"I thought they played extremely well with big plays," Dantonio said.

A negative take-away for the Spartans, however, was the special teams repeat of poor coverage. For the second straight week, the MSU opponent had a return touchdown.

Dantonio did not hamper on the subject and acknowledged that mistakes will happen.

As for Oregon's performance, Dantonio and Cook were quick to point out that the Ducks have great playmakers and played a good game.

The Duck's quarterback, transfer Vernon Adams Jr., finished the game with 22 completions on 39 attempts, 309 passing yards, one touchdown and two interceptions.

Adams Jr. was under pressure nearly all game and never seemed to be comfortable in the pocket. The Spartans were able to sack Adams Jr. four times and hurry him six times.

The Ducks sophomore running back Royce Freeman had 24 carries for 92 yards and one touchdown. For a player of his caliber, the Spartans' defensive line held him to a reasonable margin and their push in the trenches was a large factor in the game. ■

Right: Michigan State players say a prayer after the game against Oregon. Alice Cole/The State News Opposite: The Spartans' offensive line faces off against the Ducks' defensive line during the fourth quarter. Catherine Ferland/The State News

For Homecoming, MSU Football Looks To Both The Past And Future

By Matthew Argillander • September 30, 2015

When No. 2-ranked MSU (4-0 overall) takes the field this weekend against Purdue (1-3 overall) it will be the first Big Ten game of the season, but also something more.

Saturday marks the 100th edition of the annual Homecoming game for the Spartans.

"We talk in terms of Michigan State football and tradition and tradition around this country, Michigan State is one of those places that has a great tradition," Dantonio said. "So to be a part of this 100th Homecoming, it is special. This university has been on the map a long time. With that comes a lot of things that have been around for a long, long time. This will be one of them."

Dantonio's Homecoming history

Dantonio is 7-1 in Homecoming games since he came to MSU. His teams have outscored their opponents 266-149 in those games per msuspartans.com.

- **Game 1:** Oct. 13, 2007 MSU defeated Indiana 52-27.

- **Game 2:** Oct. 4, 2008 MSU defeated Iowa 16-13.

- **Game 3:** Oct. 17, 2009 MSU defeated Northwestern 24-14.

- **Game 4:** Oct. 16, 2010 MSU defeated Illinois 26-6.

- **Game 5:** Oct. 22, 2011 MSU defeated Wisconsin 37-31.

- **Game 6:** Oct. 13, 2012 MSU's lone loss under Dantonio in Homecoming games. A 19-16 loss to Iowa in double overtime.

- **Game 7:** Oct. 12, 2013 MSU defeated Indiana 42-28.

- **Game 8:** Sept. 27, 2014 MSU defeated Wyoming 56-14.

What it means

For Dantonio and his players, Homecoming is an opportunity to reunite the Spartan family and spend time with familiar faces.

"I do look forward to seeing our players when they come back," Dantonio said. Some of them come back every now and then, periodically, but for me, that's what Homecoming is. It's our players coming back. I think in a large university like this, I'm sure every segment of the university has people coming back and it's special for me."

For junior linebacker Riley Bullough, Homecoming is an opportunity to hear from the former Spartans who laid the foundation for today's success.

"Homecoming means a lot," Bullough said. "We're going to have a lot of former teammates here that we'll see, former friends and the teammates that set the foundation for our program and how it is now. Whenever we can see them and have them speak to us it means a lot."

Senior defensive end Shilique Calhoun is taking it one game at a time. He admitted that it is hard not to think about his time coming to an end.

"I just try to embrace my friends, embrace the moments instead of focusing on (the fact)

The Spartan Marching Band performs at Spartan Stadium before MSU's September 20, 2014, game against Eastern Michigan. Julia Nagy/The State News

"I just try to embrace my friends, embrace the moments instead of focusing on (the fact) that my time is deteriorating here." — Senior defensive end Shilique Calhoun

that my time is deteriorating here," Calhoun said. "I try to embrace each and every day, embrace the practices that we have, but there's always going to be that time clock in my head."

Calhoun said he didn't realize how special Homecoming is until just recently. He also talked about how special it is to be playing in the 100th edition of the game likening it to playing in and winning the 100th edition of the Rose Bowl.

"I don't think I realized Homecoming was such a big game until this year," Calhoun said. "It's such a big moment, a lot of the alumni to come back to experience that college life again and witness a game or to be on campus again. ...I think it's going to be a sad moment (for me), but at the same time if we get a win, I'll be pretty happy."

The weekend will also serve as an opportunity for MSU to welcome the 1965-'66 team back to campus. The 1965-'66 team will be honored at halftime and the 1990 Big Ten Championship Team will also be in East Lansing for their 25 year reunion.

The matchup

Purdue is a team that has always played MSU tough, but that is unlikely this year.

Purdue opened the season with a 10-point loss to Marshall. In week three they suffered a lopsided 51-24 loss to Virginia Tech and just last week they were defeated by MAC opponent Bowling Green.

The Spartan Stadium student section cheers on the Spartans during MSU's game against Western Michigan in August 2013. Opposite: The marching band holds Spartan flags during MSU's game against Youngstown State in September 2013. Julia Nagy/The State News

"The Big Ten play is what we preach about all offseason and Purdue, a quality opponent who's played us tough, is the first stepping stone to getting to Indianapolis." — Junior linebacker Riley Bullough

The Boilermakers only win this season came against FCS opponent Indiana State.

The Spartans won't look past the Boilermakers because it is an important step toward their ultimate goals of winning a Big Ten Championship and a national championship.

"The Big Ten play is what we preach about all offseason and Purdue, a quality opponent who's played us tough, is the first stepping stone to getting to Indianapolis," Bullough said.

For senior center Jack Allen, the team's long-term goals start with short-term goals.

"You've got to get (to the Big Ten Championship) to get to the next step," Allen said. "I've always been a person that hasn't looked past anyone or anything, you just take it a step at a time and right now our goal is just to win our side of the conference and we're taking it a week at a time."

Allen said with Big Ten play things get a bit more intense and ultimately this is what some guys came to MSU to do.

"I'm excited about it, it's fun playing teams you don't usually play," Allen said. "But, at the same time we came here to play and we want to play some Big Ten teams. Everything is going to get amped up this week." ∎

Right: The Spartan Marching Band and the student section cheer during a September 2014 home game against Eastern Michigan. Erin Hampton/The State News Opposite: The Spartans celebrate with Sparty after MSU's 56-14 win over Wyoming on September 27, 2014. Julia Nagy/The State News

Cook On Wild Victory: "Honestly, It Just Felt Like A Dream"

By Matthew Argillander • October 17, 2015

No. 7-ranked MSU defeated No. 12-ranked Michigan 27-23 in what could go down as the craziest college football game of the year.

With 10 seconds left on the clock and the game all but over, Michigan's senior punter Blake O'Neill muffed the snap and sophomore defensive back Jalen Watts-Jackson took it all the way to the house to give the Spartans a win.

Here are a few takeaways from the game.

Special teams

Aside from the final play of the game, MSU's special teams were awful and nearly cost the Spartans their undefeated season.

Backup quarterback Tyler O'Connor was forced to punt most of the game and it wasn't pretty.

The Spartans finished the game with just 23.6 net yards per punt. The punting unit was so shaky that head coach Mark Dantonio felt the need to fake a punt from his own 38, the failed attempt lead to a Michigan touchdown and looked as if it would be the most important play of the game.

The team's lack of trust in junior kicker Michael Geiger was evident as the Spartans chose to go for it multiple times from what would be field goal position for a lot of teams.

Loss for words

Dantonio, who was dancing in the locker room with his players before coming out to address the media, often struggled to put what his team accomplished into words.

"Great, great, great football game," Dantonio said. "I don't know what to say about that, you go from 10 seconds (left) and the guy punting the ball, thinking okay this is done and all of a sudden life gets flipped upside down."

Crazy finish

Senior quarterback Connor Cook was just hoping for a chance to get a play off at the end of the game.

The Spartans plan for the final play of the game if the Wolverines successfully punted it? Lateral and score a touchdown. So, in short the game was over.

Cook admitted that he was hoping Watts-Jackson would get tackled so they could attempt a field goal to win the game, but when he saw him getting closer and the clock hit 0:00 he figured "he might as well just score a touchdown and jump into the endzone."

"Honestly, it just felt like a dream," Cook said. "I was running over to our student and parent section to go celebrate with my family and I jumped up there and honestly I've never felt anything like that."

Cook would later say that the feeling of this win topped his feelings that came with the wins in the Rose Bowl and Cotton Bowl.

Final notes

Dantonio admitted in the press conference following the game that he wished he would have punted on the late 4th and 19 with two timeouts left instead of calling his second timeout to draw up a play.

At the time that use of a timeout seemed like a bad decision, but if things were done differently the result could have been different as well.

The last play of the game was bitter-sweet as the man who made the play, Watts-Jackson, injured his hip on the return. Dantonio speculated that it was either a dislocated or broken hip. ■

Junior tight end Josiah Price, 82, and the rest of the MSU football team celebrates in the end zone after redshirt freshman defensive back Jalen Watts-Jackson ran the ball in for the game-winning touchdown against Michigan. Joshua Abraham/The State News

ESPN's Most-Watched 3:30 p.m. Game Of All Time

By Ryan Kryska • October 23, 2015

The MSU game against University of Michigan on Saturday was ESPN's most-watched 3:30 p.m. game of all time. The game was also ESPN's most-watched college football game in October since the Florida State-Miami game in 1994 , according to Spartan Athletics.

On average, 7.4 million viewers tuned in for the Spartans vs. Wolverines game, and in the nine minutes surrounding the final play, the number of people tuned in grew to 11.5 million, according to Spartan Athletics.

The game was also WatchESPN's second-most viewed game of all time with 697,000 visitors spending 39.4 million minutes on its network, according to Spartan Athletics.

The Spartans vs. Wolverines game was the sixth most-watched game of the season, with the top five all being Saturday night games, according to Spartan Athletics. The top game was Ohio State vs. Virginia Tech on Sept. 7 with 10.6 million views and the Spartans' game against Oregon was the third most with 7.9 million viewers.

OSU, University of Alabama and MSU are the only three schools to have more than one game on the season's most-watched list, with OSU and Alabama recording three games, according to Spartan Athletics. ■

Right: Michigan safety and kick return man Jabrill Peppers (5) tries to fight past Spartans sophomore linebacker Chris Frey (23). Frey finished with four tackles on the day. Alice Kole/The State News Opposite: Sophomore defensive back Jalen Watts-Jackson runs the ball for the game-winning touchdown as time expired during the game against Michigan. Joshua Abraham/The State News

MSU Keeps Playoff Hopes Alive With Win Over Ohio State

By Matthew Argillander • November 22, 2015

Before the 2015 football season began, many Spartan fans had Nov. 21 circled on their calendars. In a season full of lofty expectations, MSU knew the game against Ohio State would be the most important of the season.

Then-No. 9 MSU (10-1 overall, 6-1 Big Ten) upset then-No. 3 Ohio State (10-1 overall, 6-1 Big Ten), 17-14, off a 41-yard field goal from junior kicker Michael Geiger, silencing a record-breaking crowd at Ohio Stadium of 108,975 people.

"Last February when we started winter conditioning we talked about reaching higher, and one of the ways we needed to reach higher was to come in here and win," head coach Mark Dantonio said. "We focused on this moment and we played hard."

How it Happened

With Connor Cook all but guaranteeing his starting status for the game throughout the week, it came as a shock to many as game time approached that it wasn't Cook taking a majority of snaps in pre-game warmups, but backup quarterbacks sophomore Damion Terry and junior Tyler O'Connor.

When Cook did take snaps in warmup with the first team, it was apparent something was not right. Most of his passes were softly lofted over the middle of the field, not showing his usual ability to put any power behind his throws.

When the Spartans took the field, they were without their quarterback who had started 36 consecutive games and compiled a record of 32-4 over that span. Instead, Dantonio opted for a dual-quarterback system with O'Connor handling most of the passing plays. One thing was for sure — without Cook, the defense would need to be dominant for the Spartans to have a shot against the Buckeyes.

The Spartans dominated OSU on both sides of the ball to end the Buckeyes' 23-game winning streak and 30-game winning streak in regular season conference games. The Spartans were 13-point underdogs.

"Huge win for our program, if you really look at it we sat around all day and listened to how we were underdogs and I think that motivates people," Dantonio said. "I think this is the first game we've played all season long where we could actually take on the role as the people who were underdogs and hunting that other football team.

"We came in with something to prove, usually when you have that you have a chip on your shoulder and you play a little bit better."

Buckeyes star running back Ezekiel Elliott had an FBS-leading streak of 15 consecutive games with at least 100 rushing yards coming into the game.

The Spartans held Elliott to just 33 yards on 12 carries with an average of 2.8 yards per carry, a stark contrast from his season average of 6.5 yards per carry.

"We tackled well, we won at the line of scrimmage," Dantonio said. "There wasn't a lot

Linebacker Darien Harris takes down Ohio State running back Ezekiel Elliott in the second quarter of the Spartans' 17-14 win over the Buckeyes. Julia Nagy/The State News

"Obviously we've gone through some adversity up front, but I think this week we truly gelled as an offensive front and as an offense. We just need to continue to do what we're doing and keep believing in what we thought we could do all year." — Senior center Jack Allen

of places (for Elliott) to go."

Coming into the game match up, MSU had only allowed a total of three points scored off of turnovers. All 14 of Ohio State's points came from two Spartan turnovers.

The first turnover came off of a sack-fumble on MSU quarterback Damion Terry for the Buckeyes' Sam Hubbard. OSU then went on a 10-play, 32-yard touchdown drive capped off by an Elliott touchdown run.

The second turnover came on a muffed punt by Macgarrett Kings Jr. that the Buckeyes recovered at MSU's 6-yard line. OSU scored on the very next play with a touchdown pass from J.T. Barrett to Jalin Marshall.

Overall, MSU held the Buckeyes to just 132 yards of total offense — 321 yards less than their season average of 453.

The Spartans forced six OSU three-and-outs and held them to 4-of-14 on third down conversions. MSU also dominated the time of possession battle with 38:10 compared to 21:50 for the Buckeyes. OSU was forced to punt on nine of their 11 drives, the only two non-punts were the two that came from turnovers.

"Two (backup) quarterbacks went in and did an excellent job, didn't flinch," Dantonio said. "I think it's important that as a football program you overachieve and I think we did that."

High stakes

Whenever the Spartans and Buckeyes play there is a lot on the line. In 2013, MSU defeated a previously undefeated OSU team in the Big Ten championship. Had the Buckeyes won they would have been headed to the BCS National championship.

That victory in the Big Ten championship ended a school-record winning streak of 24 games for the Buckeyes.

Last season, OSU came into East Lansing and defeated a then-No. 8 MSU team. The Buckeyes would go on to secure a berth in the inaugural College Football Playoffs where they defeated Alabama and Oregon en route to a national championship.

In 2015, the Spartans' win over the Buckeyes likely ended OSU's playoff hopes and rekindled MSU's. OSU head coach Urban Meyer's record stood at 29-0 against other Big Ten teams and 2-2 against MSU.

"Real excited for our football team and our program," Dantonio said. "We cannot lose sight. We have to win next week, we at least control our own destiny and that's the goal." ■

Spartans kicker Michael Geiger kicks the game-winning field goal against Ohio State. Geiger's 41-yard field silenced a record-breaking crowd of 108,975 at Ohio Stadium.
Julia Nagy/The State News

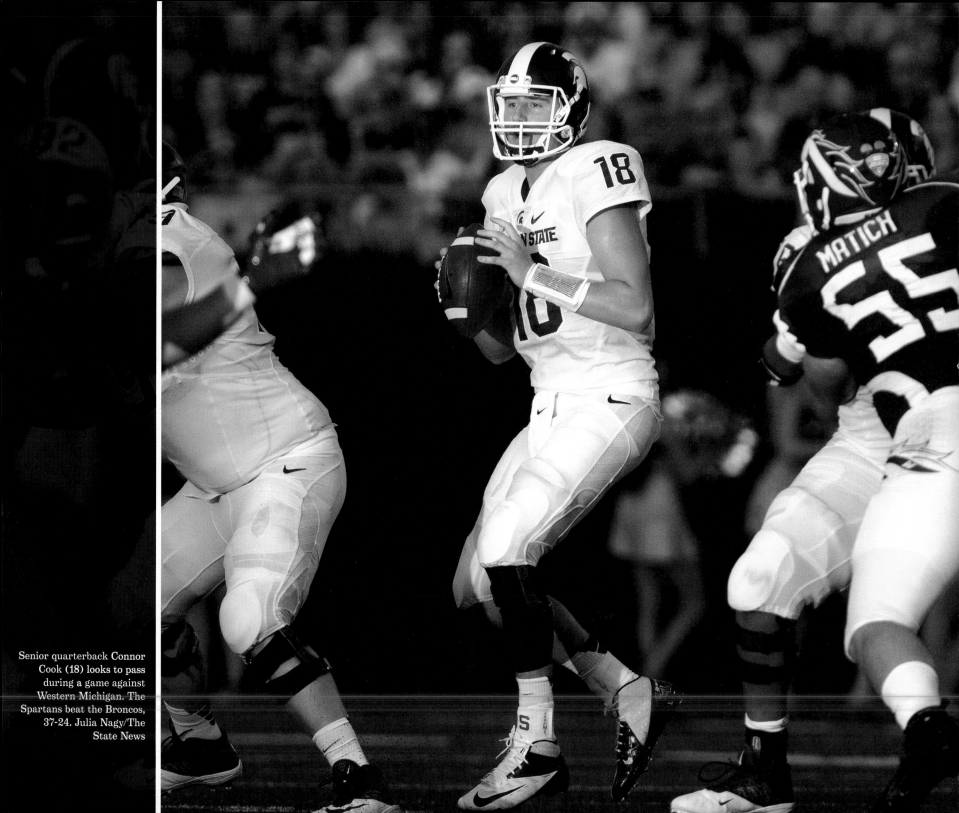

Senior quarterback Connor Cook (18) looks to pass during a game against Western Michigan. The Spartans beat the Broncos, 37-24. Julia Nagy/The State News

Cook Taking His Place As Best Quarterback In Spartan History

By Matthew Argillander • November 15, 2015

What do pro-style quarterbacks Jeff Driskel, Cody Kessler, Max Wittek, Christian LeMay, Brandon Allen, David Ash, Kyle Boehm, Reilly O'Toole, Tony McNeal, Chad Jeffries, Gary Nova and Cardale Jones all have in common?

They were all ranked ahead of MSU senior quarterback Connor Cook in the 2011 recruiting cycle.

Cook, who has emerged as one of the top quarterbacks in the country, was unranked nationally and very underrated coming out of Walsh Jesuit High School in Cuyahoga Falls, Ohio.

"I think Connor kind of started with a little bit of a chip on his shoulder, a little bit of an edge psychologically and competitively, because he wasn't as highly regarded as these four-star or five-star recruits coming out," Hall of Fame MSU quarterback Jimmy Raye II said. "I think that it served him well, I think the way he goes about his business and his competitive nature, I think that intangible gives him a big edge in terms of the way he performs."

Cook was born to be an athlete. His father Chris played tight end at Indiana, his mother Donna played basketball at Cincinnati and his sister Jackie played basketball at Old Dominion.

The senior signal-caller for the Spartans is the perfect player for head coach Mark Dantonio. He is the embodiment of the chip that Dantonio has been talking about, considering his father's alma mater Indiana didn't even offer him a scholarship.

How it started

Dec. 29, 2012 is a day Spartan fans should remember forever. After a disappointing 2012 regular season with Andrew Maxwell under center for the Spartans, MSU found itself trailing Texas Christian in the Buffalo Wild Wings Bowl and Dantonio gave everyone their first glimpse at the man who would take the program to the next level after some recent success.

Cook went on to lead MSU to a 17-16 victory over TCU that night and he never looked back. Cook officially won the starting job four games into the 2013 season after splitting reps with Maxwell during the first three games.

However, he began to face doubt after a slow start to that year.

Through four games, MSU was 3-1 with the offense struggling to find a rhythm against weaker opponents in Western Michigan and South Florida. The Spartans also lost a close contest to Notre Dame in Cook's debut as the No. 1 quarterback.

The Spartans would go on to win every game the rest of that season including a 24-20 win over Stanford in the final BCS edition of the Rose Bowl.

Cook, the winningest quarterback in MSU history, has only lost three more games in the season and a half since, for a total career record of 32-4.

"It's very comforting having a quarterback like that, having a leader like that in Connor Cook," sophomore linebacker Jon Reschke said. "He really helps out our defense, because we can always rely on him making big plays, making those third down conversions."

Some may argue that Cook had a great defense to carry him and there is no denying the

talent of MSU's defense especially in 2013, but he's led the Spartans to several big victories.

Cook has shown a unique ability to find a way to win — trailing Baylor 41-28 with about 12 minutes left in the 2014 Cotton Bowl the Spartans had just recovered an onside kick and momentum appeared to be on their side.

On the first play of the drive Cook hit Aaron Burbridge for 39 yards to the Baylor 14, but on the very next play he threw an ugly interception that looked like it would be the death of MSU.

Proving his ability to shake off mistakes, Cook led the Spartans to two straight touchdown drives of nine plays and 60 yards and eight plays and 81 yards to win 42-41 in stunning come-from-behind fashion.

The greatest ever

Cook has the MSU record with 68 passing touchdowns, he's tied for the most 300-yard passing games and he needs just 314 more yards to become the leader in total offense — his 8,775 yards of total offense trails just Kirk Cousins (9,004) and recently overtook Jeff Smoker (8,714) on Saturday .

But it's not just the stats. Cook arguably has the most tools of any quarterback to come through MSU, and he could be a first-round pick in the next NFL draft.

"He's used to being successful, so he has confidence. He's able to take a bad play and flip it, play through it and come out the back end playing very well," Dantonio said. "He could have a poor first quarter and play lights out three quarters in a row. It's not going to bother him. He's got a lot of control of the offense. He's shown great leadership in the huddle and great leadership on the field.

"[His skills] are NFL-type level from what I know. The NFL quarterbacks that we've had here, I would say he's right there with those guys. He's got a great touch, he's got great arm strength, he's got a very quick release, and he's big."

If you take a minute to watch Cook on game-day, he's completing throws many college quarterbacks in the country wouldn't even attempt — threading the needle and splitting defenders, long passes down the field to his receivers in stride and perfect throws that are put where only his receiver can make a play.

The last quarterback to lead the Spartans to a national championship, Raye, had high praise for Cook.

"(I would rank Connor Cook) at the very top, he followed an outstanding quarterback at Michigan State — Kirk Cousins," Raye said. "I think he has taken what Kirk brought (MSU) what Michigan State was able to accomplish while Kirk was there and I think he's taken it to new heights and another level.

It doesn't take Raye to realize what Cook has done for MSU in his time as the starter. Cook did what most of the other greats couldn't, he led the Spartans to their first Rose Bowl win since 1988, he's the winningest quarterback in MSU history and he has MSU in contention for another big time bowl game or possibly a playoff spot with some help.

"Of all the great quarterbacks that Michigan State has had going back to the days of Earl Morrall, Albert Dorow, Jim Ninowski ... Brian Hoyer and Drew Stanton, I think going back through all of those guys he'll be at the very top." ■

Connor Cook throws a pass while junior tight end Josiah Price (82) blocks Air Force outside linebacker Ryan Watson (40), during the Spartans 35-21 win over the Falcons.
Joshua Abraham/The State News

MSU Defeats Iowa 16-13, Likely Advances To College Football Playoff

By Ryan Kryska • December 5, 2015

MSU football defeated Iowa in dramatic fashion in the Big Ten Football championship game, 16-13. A touchdown from freshman running back L.J. Scott from 1-yard out with 27 seconds remaining clinched the victory.

The Spartans advance to 12-1 on the season and likely clinch themselves a spot in the College Football Playoff.

The atmosphere at Lucas Oil Stadium shifted toward Iowa on the first play of the fourth quarter.

This is because the play was also the first touchdown of the game and because it was an 85-yard reception — the 2015 Spartan fans' biggest fear.

Iowa junior quarterback C.J. Beathard threw the pass to senior wide receiver Trevaun Smith and he took it the distance. The Hawkeye's took the lead 13-9 just over 10 seconds into the fourth quarter.

MSU's next possession stalled, and when Iowa got the ball back with 12:14 left, its first play was another shot deep, which was not completed but warranted a defensive holding call on the Spartans.

The Hawkeyes caught on. They were the team to break the code and turn this downhill deadlock into an advantaged schematic. But though the Spartans defense bent, they did not break.

And when MSU got the ball back, it proved to have a trick up its sleeve as well. Counters, misdirections and a wildcat offense caught Iowa over pursuing and added a needed wrinkle to the offense. Then, senior wide receiver Aaron Burbridge did what he does.

After a Burbridge catch that was overturned by review, he caught a third-down rocket from fifth-year senior Connor Cook and held onto the ball through two big hits.

Freshman running back LJ Scott continued the Spartans' late-striving drive with runs that put MSU in makeable third-down situations.

And with 2:09 remaining in the game, a media timeout gave both teams a chance to game plan as MSU had the ball at the Iowa 10-yard line for a second-and-seven.

Scott carried the ball for five yards, bringing the ball to the 5-yard line, and Iowa called its first timeout as MSU faced a third-and-two.

Scott carried the ball for no gain, giving MSU a fourth-and-two with 1:59 remaining and Iowa called its second timeout.

Cook carried for an undetermined amount of yards and the chain gang measured ~ it was

Head coach Mark Dantonio and the MSU football coaching staff watches a play during the Big Ten championship game against Iowa at Lucas Oil Stadium in Indianapolis. The Spartans defeated the Hawkeyes 16-13 to claim the Big Ten crown. Alice Kole/The State News

first-and-goal for MSU from the Iowa 3-yard line.

Scott carried, was literally flipped forward and downed at the 1-yard line with the clock winding under a minute.

Scott carried for no gain and MSU called a timeout with 33 seconds left.

The next play was miraculous, as Scott had contact made on him short of the goal-line, but he spun and stretched the ball across the line without fumbling to score the go-ahead touchdown with 27 seconds left.

MSU took the lead 16-13.

Iowa's desperation drive began with a fumble by Beathard for a loss of major yardage. The Hawkeyes rushed the line and spiked the ball, leaving them five seconds on the clock.

It didn't happen.

The Spartans rushed the field and defeated Iowa, 16-13, to take the Big Ten championship and likely advance to the College Football Playoff. ■

Right: Senior tight end Paul Lang looks up field after catching a pass from quarterback Connor Cook. Lang's lone catch on the day went for 17 yards in the close win vs Iowa. Opposite: Freshman running back LJ Scott (3) reaches over the goal line for the game-winning touchdown against the Hawkeyes, which propelled the Spartans to their first ever appearance in the College Football Playoff. Julia Nagy/The State News

MSU Football's Miraculous 2015 Journey Continues With The College Football Playoff

By Ryan Kryska • December 6, 2015

When freshman running back LJ Scott scored MSU's game-winning touchdown during MSU's Big Ten championship victory over Iowa Saturday night , a 6-foot-2 and 268-pound Hawkeye defensive end went on a string to jostle Scott's extended arm, but Scott moved the ball at the perfect time to evade a devastating turnover and reach it over the goal line.

Twenty-seven seconds later, the MSU players stormed the field, reaching their helmets high into the air to celebrate a 16-13 victory over Iowa. They knew what this win meant — a College Football Playoff spot — and the eventual selection on Sunday proved this true as No. 3 MSU (12-1) will be playing No. 2 Alabama (12-1) in the national semifinals — the Cotton Bowl, which the Spartans won last year over Baylor 42-41.

"We knew we had to execute each play," Scott said. "You know, we knew each play was big and that we had to stay with the ball. I was just trying to make a big play for my brothers. We knew what we had at stake."

Team of destiny

What awaits MSU now is quite possibly the most successful program of the decade — Alabama, a team coached by former-MSU head coach Nick Saban . During his years at MSU from 1995-99, Saban went 34-24-1 and left before the 1999 team's Citrus Bowl game to become the coach at LSU.

MSU is one of seven universities out of the 128 NCAA Division I teams to have been selected for the College Football Playoff since its institution last year. The 2015 Spartans football team is the first in MSU history to play in the new format and has a chance at the national championship for the first time since 1966.

MSU Athletics Director Mark Hollis, on the field minutes after the game, said MSU's current position makes this team feel like one of destiny.

MSU defeated Iowa, 16-13 to win the 2015 Big Ten Championship.

"It sort of does (feel like destiny) and there are so many special kids on this team that you just embrace them every time you have a situation like this," Hollis said. "Our goal is always to enter every season with these expectations and when you can have the conclusion end up this way it demonstrates that it is not just lip service, it is something that we feel we have the right coaches, we have a great

Senior linebacker Darien Harris kisses the Big 10 football championship trophy after MSU defeated the Iowa, 16-13. Julia Nagy/The State News

"**Our goal is always to enter every season with these expectations and when you can have the conclusion end up this way it demonstrates that it is not just lip service, it is something that we feel we have the right coaches, we have a great president a fan base and our student-athletes have a relationship with their coaches that is just unbelievable.**" — Mark Hollis

president and fan base and our student-athletes have a relationship with their coaches that is just unbelievable."

Knowing a berth was solidified, MSU fans in Lucas Oil Stadium rushed in a frenzy to the front row railings. Members and allegiances of the MSU program joined the team on the field and the Big Ten championship stage was promptly setup near the visiting sideline.

Fifth-year senior quarterback Connor Cook was named Big Ten championship game MVP after a day of completing 50 percent of his passes and running for a crucial fourth-and-two, which forced Cook to dive forward with his hurt right shoulder.

"Obviously I wasn't 100 percent," Cook said. "I got a grit it out being in a situation like this, playing for a championship. You have to go out there and compete."

Head coach Mark Dantonio spoke victorious words and was recognized as a Big Ten champion for the third time at MSU.

"We started out today and wanted to go a little bit farther than we did last year, 12-1 and we're marching, we're marching," Dantonio said. "I can't say enough how proud we are to be Spartans.

"It's a special time, with special people at a special place."

Right: From left to right, junior wide receiver R.J. Shelton, junior cornerback Jermaine Edmondson and senior defensive end Shilique Calhoun celebrate after the Big Ten championship game. Opposite: Defensive tackle Craig Evans wears the confetti in Indianapolis. Julia Nagy/The State News

Sparty's heroes

All the while, the University of Michigan game hero, redshirt freshman defensive back Jalen Watts-Jackson was leaning on his crutches, standing dead-center of the green and white end zone.

His head was on a swivel as teammates danced around with blue, red, orange and yellow confetti trailing from their shoulder pads.

"It's a blessing to be here with my team you know, just to see that everything paid off and everything worked out," Watts-Jackson said. "This was always our goal, just to be here, and it is just a blessing."

The trophy presentation ended, but the celebration continued. Watts-Jackson's fellow punt-block "Ranger" and freshman safety Grayson Miller was awestruck by what he called his team's fourth miraculous finish in just his 13th career game.

"Oh my God, this is the craziest feeling I have ever had," Miller said.

Across the field, the game's top scorer, junior kicker Michael Geiger, could be seen smiling at the crowd lined up above the tunnel as he walked into the locker room. Geiger made a 41-yard field goal against Ohio State to keep MSU's playoff hopes alive.

"I'm feeling unbelievable," said Geiger, who made field goals from 23, 29 and 47 yards during the game. "Awesome trip, but it's not done yet, we

Right: Head coach Mark Dantonio holds up the Big Ten championship trophy. Opposite: The Spartans celebrate with fans after the big win in Indianapolis. Alice Kole/The State News

still have all our goals in front of us, incredibly. This is one big step definitely and I am just looking forward to seeing what we can do in the final four."

And Geiger was right, because MSU will be playing meaningful football on Dec. 31.

"So, we are where we want this program but you never, you never want to take a rest, you got to keep it pushing and you want to be back here every year," Hollis said.

Not done yet

The Spartans' next opponent, Alabama, has been in the top four in the CFP since the rankings were released in week nine and have been No. 2 since week 10 . The Crimson Tide defeated Florida, 29-15 , in the SEC championship game on Saturday. The Cotton Bowl is scheduled to begin at 8 p.m. EST at AT&T Stadium is in Arlington, Texas.

Dantonio said he would be enjoying the Big Ten championship on Saturday, and not moving on to any potential semifinal match-ups. However, Dantonio did say something that could just be a coincidence, but still speaks to the clear brand he's built.

"Well, I just think we have resilience," Dantonio said.

Many who have followed Dantonio's team can also agree what he's built his program upon. And that includes MSU human biology junior Blake Feighner, who stood in amazement and watched the entirety of the postgame celebrations.

"It means resiliency," Feighner said. "It means being a team that is not supposed to be there. I've been a State fan for a while. I was a part of a fan base when I'd be happy at a bowl game, I'd be happy at six wins, I'd be happy at seven wins and now at this point we settle for nothing but a national championship and that is what I love about this program and that is what I love about Mark Dantonio." ■

Right: Senior defensive end Shilique Calhoun motions after making a tackle in the third quarter against the Hawkeyes. Opposite: Head coach Mark Dantonio cradles the trophy after Michigan State's win over Iowa in the Big Ten championship game. Julia Nagy/The State News

Despite Disappointing Loss In Cotton Bowl, MSU Football's Future Is Bright

By Matthew Argillander • January 10, 2016

The season might have ended in a disappointing loss for the MSU football team, but for legendary Spartan running back Clinton Jones, a member of the last national championship team in 1966, this past season gives the program credibility.

"We have a winning program, period," Jones said. "Our results speak for themselves... In the time that Mark Dantonio has been there, we've been on track for nothing but one success after another."

When asked to compare his championship winning teams to head coach Mark Dantonio's 2015 edition of the Spartans, Jones said this year's group is "the best of the 21st century" and people can't really compare them because it is two different generations of football.

"They are setting their own legacy," Jones said. "This administration, from Lou Anna K. Simon to Mark Hollis to Mark Dantonio and his staff and Tom Izzo with basketball, they've done an amazing job and I'm so proud of them."

Despite the lopsided 38-0 loss to Alabama in the College Football Playoff, Jones believes MSU has a program built to last and used the words of legendary football coach Vince Lombardi to describe what he believes is the next step for the Spartans.

"Vince Lombardi has a saying, he said that 'the real glory goes to the person that's knocked down on their knees and gets up,'" Jones said. "And so they were knocked down to their knees in the playoff game against Alabama, but they will rise. If a young man is swayed because of the loss to Alabama, they don't need to be a part of our program anyway."

Looking forward

So what is next for the Spartans?

In the short term, they have a very solid team on paper next year. Defensive impact players such as junior middle linebacker Riley Bullough, sophomore outside linebacker Jon Reschke and sophomore defensive lineman Malik McDowell will be returning next season. Also, fifth-year senior linebacker Ed Davis should be returning if the NCAA grants him a medical redshirt as expected.

MSU has a favorable schedule next year, aside from a week three matchup at Notre Dame after a bye week. The Spartans will host University of Wisconsin, Ohio State University and University of Michigan in the 2016 season, along with Brigham Young University and Northwestern.

MSU's defense should be good enough to keep them in any game next season. The bigger

Junior quarterback Tyler O'Connor runs the ball in the fourth quarter during Michigan State's upset at Ohio State on Nov. 21, 2015. Julia Nagy/The State News

question is whether the guy under center will be good enough to steal the close wins.

In the 2012 season MSU had a talented defense, but ineffective quarterback play by Andrew Maxwell led to several close losses. The 2012 edition of the Spartans went 7-6, losing to Notre Dame, Ohio State, Iowa and a "Hoke-era" U-M team, among others. Five of MSU's losses were by a combined 13 points.

They were a powerful team, but they didn't have a quarterback that could lead them down the field in the two-minute drill, or a quarterback that could get the first down to eat the rest of the clock up and win the game.

So really the question is — who between Tyler O'Connor and Damion Terry is going to be the guy that wins the close ones in 2016?

"They've had plenty of reps in practice," senior quarterback Connor Cook said.

"They know the offense just as good as me. So they're experienced guys. Tyler is going to be a senior next year. Damion is going to be a junior. So those guys what they're going to take with them going into next year is just the experience and knowledge of the offense and just the familiarity and comfort that they have.

"Obviously, they have the experience from playing in the Ohio State game. Playing on the road at the Shoe, that's hard to win at, and they won there. They can take that game away."

The long haul

In the long term, MSU seems like a program built to contend both nationally and in the Big Ten for years to come. Dantonio has routinely turned two- and three-star recruits into top-notch players. But he now has more at his disposal.

The 2015 recruiting class, which finished ranked No. 22 nationally on Yahoo's rivals.com, featured instant playmakers like freshman running back LJ Scott and freshman linebacker Andrew Dowell and it was considered one of MSU's best ever.

The recruits in the 2016 cycle could be even better — the young players across the nation have taken notice of what Dantonio is doing in East Lansing.

The 2016 recruiting class is ranked No. 12 on Yahoo's rivals.com and features five commits who will play in the Army All-American game — wide receiver Cameron Chambers, wide receiver Donnie Corley, linebacker Brandon Randle, defensive end Joshua King and defensive back Demetric Vance — along with highly-touted quarterback recruit Messiah deWeaver.

"They reached higher goals like they set out to do early in the season so it meant a lot (for them) to get to that point," deWeaver said.

"I think a lot of kids in the next class in 2017 and on will see Michigan State as one of the elite programs.... We have a lot of kids in our class that are All-Americans and some of the higher (rated) kids in the country so I think it's only going to get better."

The Spartans have several players starring in the NFL right now, such as running back Le'Veon Bell and quarterbacks Kirk Cousins and Brian Hoyer, both who led their respective teams to the playoffs. There could be more to come — Cook, Shilique Calhoun and Jack Conklin have all been mentioned as possible first round draft picks.

Players such as Darqueze Dennard and Trae Waynes are recent first round selections. The recruits have noticed the amount of talent Dantonio is sending to the next level and they want the same thing.

"It says a lot about that staff and what they can do," deWeaver said. "It just shows you that they know what they're doing. ... I think it says a lot about how great of coaches they are."

MSU's 65 wins since 2010 are tied for fourth most among NCAA Football Bowl Subdivision teams and Dantonio and his staff are recruiting some of the most talented young players MSU has ever seen. So if you're asking for a forecast of the future of MSU football, it's bright. ■

Junior linebacker Riley Bullough tries to tackle Alabama quarterback Jake Coker in the third quarter of Michigan State's loss to Alabama in the 2015 Cotton Bowl. Bullough is one of Michigan State's top returning players in 2016. Julia Nagy/The State News

Mark Dantonio Through The Years

2007 Season

Date	Opponent	MSU AP Rank	Site	Result
September 1	UAB		Home	W 55-18
September 8	Bowling Green		Home	W 28-17
September 15	Pittsburgh		Home	W 17-13
September 22	at Notre Dame		Away	W 31-14
September 29	at #9 Wisconsin		Away	L 34-37
October 6	Northwestern		Home	L 41-48 OT
October 13	Indiana		Home	W 52-27
October 20	at #1 Ohio State		Away	L 17-24
October 27	at Iowa		Away	L 27-34 2OT
November 3	#14 Michigan		Home	L 24-28
November 10	at Purdue		Away	W 48-31
November 17	#22 Penn State		Home	W 35-31
December 28	vs #14 Boston College		Champs Sports Bowl	L 21-24

Overall Record	Conference Record	Big Ten Standings	Season End AP Rank
7-6	3-5	tied for 7th	

2009 Season

Date	Opponent	MSU AP Rank	Site	Result
September 5	Montana State		Home	W 44-3
September 12	Central Michigan		Home	L 27-29
September 19	at Notre Dame		Away	L 30-33
September 26	at Wisconsin		Away	L 30-38
October 3	#22 Michigan		Home	W 26-20 OT
October 10	at Illinois		Away	W 24-14
October 17	Northwestern		Home	W 24-14
October 24	#6 Iowa		Home	L 13-15
October 31	at Minnesota		Away	L 34-42
November 7	Western Michigan		Home	W 49-14
November 14	at Purdue		Away	W 40-37
November 21	#14 Penn State		Home	L 14-42
January 2	vs Texas Tech		Alamo Bowl	L 31-41

Overall Record	Conference Record	Big Ten Standings	Season End AP Rank
6-7	4-4	Tied for 6th	

2011 Season

Date	Opponent	MSU AP Rank	Site	Result
September 2	Youngstown State	#17	Home	W 28-6
September 10	Florida Atlantic	#17	Home	W 44-0
September 17	at Notre Dame	#15	Away	L 13-31
September 24	Central Michigan		Home	W 45-7
October 1	at Ohio State		Away	W 10-7
October 15	#11 Michigan	#23	Home	W 28-14
October 22	#4 Wisconsin	#15	Home	W 37-31
October 29	at #13 Nebraska	#9	Away	L 3-24
November 5	Minnesota	#15	Home	W 31-24
November 12	at Iowa	#13	Away	W 37-21
November 19	Indiana	#12	Away	W 55-3
November 26	at Northwestern	#11	Away	W 31-17
December 3	vs #15 Wisconsin	#11	Big 10 Championship	L 39-42
January 2	vs #18 Georgia	#12	Outback Bowl	W 33-30 3 OT

Overall Record	Conference Record	Big Ten Standings	Season End AP Rank
11-3	7-1	1st Legends Division	#11

2008 Season

Date	Opponent	MSU AP Rank	Site	Result
August 30	at California		Away	L 31-38
September 6	Eastern Michigan		Home	W 42-10
September 13	Florida Atlantic		Home	W 17-0
September 20	Notre Dame		Home	W 23-7
September 27	at Indiana		Away	W 42-29
October 4	Iowa		Home	W 16-13
October 11	at Northwestern	#23	Away	W 37-20
October 18	#12 Ohio State	#20	Home	L 7-45
October 25	at Michigan		Away	W 35-21
November 1	Wisconsin	#22	Home	W 25-24
November 8	Purdue	#18	Home	W 21-7
November 22	at #7 Penn State	#17	Away	L 18-49
January 1	vs #16 Georgia	#19	Capital One Bowl	L 12-24

Overall Record	Conference Record	Big Ten Standings	Season End AP Rank
9-4	6-2	3rd	#24

2010 Season

Date	Opponent	MSU AP Rank	Site	Result
September 4	Western Michigan		Home	W 38-14
September 11	vs Florida Atlantic		Neutral at Detroit	W 30-17
September 18	Notre Dame		Home	W 34-31 OT
September 25	Northern Colorado	#25	Home	W 45-7
October 2	#11 Wisconsin	#24	Home	W 34-24
October 9	at #18 Michigan	#17	Away	W 34-17
October 16	Illinois	#13	Home	W 26-6
October 23	at Northwestern	#8	Away	W 35-27
October 30	at #18 Iowa	#5	Away	L 6-37
November 6	Minnesota	#16	Home	W 31-8
November 20	Purdue	#11	Home	W 35-31
November 27	at Penn State	#11	Away	W 28-22
January 1	vs #15 Alabama	#7	Capital One Bowl	L 7-49

Overall Record	Conference Record	Big Ten Standings	Season End AP Rank
11-2	7-1	Tied for 1st	#14

2012 Season

Date	Opponent	MSU AP Rank	Site	Result
August 31	#24 Boise State	#13	Home	W 17-13
September 8	at Central Michigan	#11	Away	W 41-7
September 15	#20 Notre Dame	#10	Home	L 3-20
September 22	Eastern Michigan	#21	Home	W 23-7
September 29	#14 Ohio State	#20	Home	L 16-17
October 6	at Indiana		Away	W 31-27
October 13	Iowa		Home	L 16-19 2 OT
October 20	at Michigan		Away	L 10-12
October 27	at Wisconsin		Away	W 16-13 OT
November 3	#21 Nebraska		Home	L 24-28
November 17	Northwestern		Home	L 20-23
November 24	at Minnesota		Away	W 26-10
December 29	vs TCU		Buffalo Wild Wings Bowl	W 17-16

Overall Record	Conference Record	Big Ten Standings	Season End AP Rank
7-6	3-5	4th Legends Division	

2013 Season

Date	Opponent	MSU AP Rank	Site	Result
August 30	Western Michigan		Home	W 26-13
September 7	South Florida		Home	W 21-6
September 14	Youngstown State		Home	W 55-17
September 21	at #22 Notre Dame		Away	L 13-17
October 5	at Iowa		Away	W 26-14
October 12	Indiana		Home	W 42-28
October 19	Purdue		Home	W 14-0
October 26	at Illinois		Away	W 42-3
November 2	#23 Michigan	#24	Home	W 29-6
November 16	at Nebraska	#14	Away	W 41-28
November 23	at Northwestern	#13	Away	W 30-6
November 30	Minnesota	#11	Home	W 14-3
December 7	vs #2 Ohio State	#10	Big 10 Championship	W 34-24
January 1	vs #5 Stanford	#4	Rose Bowl	W 24-20

Overall Record	Conference Record	Big Ten Standings	Season End AP Rank
13-1	8-0	1st Legends Division	#3

2014 Season

Date	Opponent	MSU AP Rank	Site	Result
August 29	Jacksonville State	#8	Home	W 45-7
September 6	at #3 Oregon	#7	Away	L 27-46
September 20	Eastern Michigan	#11	Home	W 73-14
September 27	Wyoming	#9	Home	W 56-14
October 4	#19 Nebraska	#10	Home	W 27-22
October 11	at Purdue	#8	Away	W 45-31
October 18	at Indiana	#8	Away	W 56-17
October 25	Michigan	#8	Home	W 35-11
November 8	#13 Ohio State	#7	Home	L 37-49
November 15	at Maryland	#12	Away	W 37-15
November 22	Rutgers	#10	Home	W 45-3
November 29	at Penn State	#10	Away	W 34-10
January 1	vs #4 Baylor	#7	Cotton Bowl	W 42-21

Overall Record	Conference Record	Big Ten Standings	Season End AP Rank
11-2	7-1	2nd East Division	#5

2015 Season

Date	Opponent	MSU AP Rank	Site	Result
September 4	at Western Michigan	#5	Away	W 37-24
September 12	#7 Oregon	#5	Home	W 31-28
September 19	Air Force	#4	Home	W 35-21
September 26	Central Michigan	#2	Home	W 30-10
October 3	Purdue	#2	Home	W 24-21
October 10	at Rutgers	#4	Away	W 31-24
October 17	at #12 Michigan	#7	Away	W 27-23
October 24	Indiana	#7	Home	W 52-26
November 7	at Nebraska	#6	Away	L 38-39
November 14	Maryland	#13	Home	W 24-7
November 21	at #2 Ohio State	#9	Away	W 17-14
November 28	Penn State	#6	Home	W 55-16
December 5	vs #4 Iowa	#5	Big 10 Championship	W 16-13
December 31	vs #2 Alabama	#3	Cotton Bowl - College Football Playoff	L 0-38

Overall Record	Conference Record	Big Ten Standings	Season End AP Rank
12-2	7-1	1st East Division	#6

DANTONIO'S overall record
at Michigan State: **87-33**

DANTONIO'S overall Big 10 conference
record at Michigan State: **52-20**